Differentiating Instruction With Menus

Chemistry

T0313394

ADVANCED-LEVEL MENUS
Grades 9–12

Differentiating Instruction With Menus

Chemistry

Laurie E. Westphal, Ed.D.

Routledge
Taylor & Francis Group

NEW YORK AND LONDON

First published in 2019 by Prufrock Press Inc.

Published 2021 by Routledge
605 Third Avenue, New York, NY 10017
2 Park Square, Milton Park, Abingdon, Oxon OX14 4RN

Routledge is an imprint of the Taylor & Francis Group, an informa business

Copyright © 2019 by Taylor & Francis Group

Cover and layout design by Allegra Denbo

ISBN 13: 978-1-0321-4332-3 (hbk)
ISBN 13: 978-1-6182-1847-6 (pbk)

DOI: 10.4324/9781003234357

CONTENTS

PART I

All About Menus and Choice

DOI: 10.4324/9781003234357-1

CHAPTER 1

Choice

"For so many reasons, it is simply the right thing to do for this age group."

—Shared by a group of secondary teachers when asked why is choice important for their students

Why Is Choice Important?

Ask any adult if he or she would prefer to choose what to do or be told what to do, and of course, he or she is going to prefer the choice. Students, especially teenagers, have these same feelings. Although they may not always stand up and demand a choice if none are present, they benefit in many ways from having them.

One benefit of choice is its ability to meet the needs of so many different students and their varied learning preferences. The Dunedin College of Education (Keen, 2001) conducted a research study on the preferred learning styles of 250 gifted students. Students were asked to rank different learning options. Of the 13 different options described to the students, only one option did not receive at least one negative response,

 DOI: 10.4324/9781003234357-2

and that was choice. Although all students have different preferences, choice is the one option that meets all students' needs. Why? Well, it takes the focus from the teacher as the decision maker and allows students to decide what is best for them. What teenager would argue against being able to do something that he or she prefers to do? When given the opportunity to choose, students are going to choose what best fits their educational needs.

"I really was not sure how my students were going to react to these choices. I didn't want the menu to be viewed as busy work when we already had so much content to cover. I was surprised (and relieved) by how well they responded [to the choices]. Now, they want to have choice in everything, which is always up for negotiation."

—English II teacher

Another benefit of choice is its ability to address different learning preferences and ultimately offer the opportunity to better assess what students understand about the content being studied. During professional development, I often ask teachers what learning preferences are most addressed in the products they provide. Not surprisingly, visual and written products top the list. These two preferences are most popular for many reasons, including ease of grading, ease of organizing and managing, and lack of supplies needed. In looking back on all of the different products my students have created, however, I noticed that most often, the tactile, kinesthetic, and verbal products provided greater depth and complexity (Komarraju, Karau, Schmeck, & Avdic, 2011). After analyzing these "noisy" products, I have come to realize that if I really want to know what my students understand, I need to allow them to show me through their learning preference—and the most common preferences of my students are not visual-written. Most students prefer tactile-kinesthetic (Dunn & Honigsfeld, 2013; Ricca, 1984; Sagan, 2010; Snyder, 1999). Because these preferences are not always addressed during whole-class instruction, teachers need a strategy that can allow students to express themselves. Using choice to offer these opportunities can help address the needs of more students in our classrooms.

Another advantage of choice is a greater sense of independence for the students (Deci, Vallerand, Pelletier, & Ryan, 1991; Patall, 2013; Robinson, Patall, & Cooper, 2008). When teachers offer choice, students design and create a product based on what they envision, rather than what their teacher envisions. When students would enter my classroom, many times they had been trained by previous teachers to produce what the teacher wanted, not what the students thought would be best. Teaching my students that what they envision could be correct (and wonderful) could be a struggle. "Is this what you want?" or "Is this right?" were popular questions as we started the school year. As we progressed, and I continued to redirect their questions back to them ("Is that what you would like to show?" or "Does that seem right to you?"), students began to ask for my approval less; they became more independent in their work. They might still need assurance, but the phrasing was different, "This is what I have so far. Can I ask for help from Joe?" or "I don't like this; I am going to pick something else." When teachers allow students choice in the products they create to show their learning, the students can develop this independence.

Increased student focus and persistence is another benefit of offering choice. When students are making choices in the activities they wish to complete, they are more focused on the learning that is needed to create their choice products (Flowerday & Schraw, 2003; Ricca, 1984). Students become engaged when they learn information that can help them develop products that they are excited about creating. Many students struggle with the purpose of the information being taught in the classroom, and this can lead to behavior problems. Students may feel disconnected from the content and lose interest (Robinson et al., 2008). Instead, students will pay closer attention to instruction when an immediate application (the student's choice product) for the knowledge being presented in class is present. If students are excited about the product, they are more focused on the content; they are less likely to be off task during instruction.

Many a great educator has referred to the idea that the best learning takes place when the students have a desire to learn. Some students have a desire to learn anything that is new to them; others do not want to learn anything unless it has interest for them. By incorporating choice activities that require the students to stretch beyond what they already know, teachers create a void which needs to be filled. This void leads to a desire to learn.

A Point to Ponder: Making Good Choices Is a Skill

"I want my students to be independent, and it can be frustrating that they just can't make decisions for themselves. I hadn't thought I might need to actually teach decision-making skills."

—Secondary study skills teacher, after
hearing me discuss choice as a skill

When we think of making a good choice as a skill, much like writing an effective paragraph or essay, it becomes easy enough to understand that we need to encourage students to make their own choices. In keeping with this analogy, students could certainly figure out how to write on their own, and perhaps even how to compose sentences and paragraphs, by modeling other examples. Imagine, however, the progress and strength of the writing produced when students are given guidance and even the most basic of instruction on how to accomplish the task. The written piece is still their own, but the quality of the finished piece is much stronger when guidance is given during the process. There is a reason why class time is spent in the AP classroom focusing on how to write an appropriate response to a document-based question (DBQ) or free-response question (FRQ). Students need to practice the skill before the big test in May. The same is true with choices; the quality of choices our high school students can make in the classroom is directly impacted by exposure and practice.

As with writing, students could make choices on their own, but when the teacher provides background knowledge and assistance, the choices become more meaningful and the products richer. All students certainly need guidance (even if our strong-willed high school students think they know it all), as the idea of choice may be new to them. Some students may only have experienced basic instructional choices, like choosing between two journal prompts or perhaps having the option of making either a poster or a PowerPoint presentation about the content being studied. Some may not have experienced even this level of choice. This lack of experience can cause frustration for both teacher and student.

Teaching Choices as a Skill

So, what is the best way to provide guidance and enable our students to develop the skill of making good choices while still allowing them to develop their individuality? First, choose the appropriate number of choices for your students. Although the goal might be to have students choose from 20 different options, teachers might start by having their students choose from three predetermined choices the first day (if they were using a game show menu, for instance, students might choose an activity from the first column). Then, after that product had been created, students could choose from another three options from another column a few days later, and perhaps from another three the following week. By breaking students' choices down, teachers reinforce how to approach or attack a more complex and/or varied choice format in the future. All students can work up to making complex choices from longer lists of options as their choice skill level increases.

Second, although our high school students feel they know everything now, they may still need guidance on how to select the option that is right for them. They may not automatically gravitate toward options without an exciting and detailed description of each choice. For the most part, students have been trained to produce what the teacher requests, which means that when given a choice, they may choose what seems to be the easiest and what the teacher most wants (then they can get to what they would prefer to be doing). This means that when the teacher discusses the different menu options, he or she must be equally as excited about each option. The discussion of the different choices must be somewhat animated and specific. For example, if the content is all very similar, the focus should be on the product: "If you want to create something you might see on YouTube, this one is for you!" or "If you want to be artistic, check this one as a maybe!" The more exposure students have to the processing the teacher provides, the more skillful they become in their choice making.

How Can Teachers Allow Choice?

"The GT students seem to get more involved in assignments when they have choice. They have so many creative ideas and the menus give them the opportunity to use them."

—Secondary social studies teacher, when asked about how student respond to having choices

When people visit a restaurant, they are all attending with the common goal of finding something on the menu to satisfy their hunger. We all hope that when students come into our classroom, they will have a hunger as well—a hunger for learning. Choice menus are a way of allowing students to choose how they would like to satisfy that hunger. At the very least, a menu is a list of choices that students use to choose an activity (or activities) they would like to complete to show their learning. At best, it is a complex system in which students are given point goals and complete different products to earn points (which are based on the levels of Bloom's revised taxonomy; Anderson & Krathwohl, 2001). These menus should have a way to incorporate a "free choice" option for those picky eaters who would like to make a special order to satisfy their learning hunger.

The next few sections provide examples of different menu formats that will be used in this book. Each menu has benefits, limitations or drawbacks, and time considerations. An explanation of the free choice option and its management will follow the information on each type of menu.

Tic-Tac-Toe Menu

"My students really enjoy the Tic-Tac-Toe menus, and I get them to stretch themselves without them realizing it."

— High school AP World Geography teacher

Description

The Tic-Tac-Toe menu (see Figure 1.1) is a well-known, commonly used menu that contains a total of eight predetermined choices and one free choice for students. These choices can range from task statements leading to product creation, complex and/or higher level processing questions, or leveled problems for solving. The choices can be created at the same level of Bloom's revised taxonomy or can be arranged in such a way to allow for the three different levels or objectives within a unit or topic. If all choices have been created at the same level of Bloom's revised taxonomy, then each choice carries the same weight for grading and has similar expectations for completion time and effort.

Benefits

Flexibility. This menu can cover either one topic in depth, three different topics, or three objectives within one content area. When this menu covers just one objective, and all tasks are from the same level of Bloom's revised taxonomy (preferably the highest), students have the option of completing three projects in a tic-tac-toe pattern, or simply picking three from the menu. When the menu covers three objectives, three different levels of Bloom's revised taxonomy, or three different learning preferences, students will need to complete a vertical or horizontal tic-tac-toe pattern only (either a vertical column or horizontal row) to be sure they have completed one activity from each objective, level, and learning style.

Figure 1.1. Tic-Tac-Toe menu example.

Stretching. When students make choices on this menu by completing a row or column based on its design, they will usually face one choice that is out of their comfort zone. This "stretch" may result from a task's level of Bloom's revised taxonomy, its product style, or its content. Students will complete this "uncomfortable" choice because they want to do the other two in that row or column.

Friendly design. Students quickly understand how to use this menu. It is nonthreatening because it does not contain points, and therefore it seems to encourage students to stretch out of their comfort zones.

Weighting. All products are equally weighted, so recording grades and maintaining paperwork are easily accomplished.

Short time period. They are intended for shorter periods of time, between 1–3 weeks based on the tasks found on the menu as well as the amount of class time allotted for students to work on the menu.

Limitations

Few topics. These menus only cover one or three topics.

Student compromise. Although this menu does allow choice, when following the guidelines of rows or columns only, the menu provides only six different ways to meet the goal. This restriction means a student will sometimes have to compromise and complete an activity he or she would not have chosen because it completes his or her tic-tac-toe. (This is not always bad, though!)

No "safety net." Because each product in this menu is recorded as its own grade, it is possible that a student could fail this menu. Other formats allow students to make a poor choice and still earn full credit by completing additional options.

Time Considerations

Tic-Tac-Toe menus usually are intended for shorter amounts of completion time—at the most, they could take up to 3 weeks with students working outside of class and submitting one product each week. If a menu focuses on one topic in-depth and the students have time in class to work on their products, the menu could be completed in one week.

Meal Menu

"Seemed pretty easy at first—after all it was only three things and I was thinking I would just have to draw a few equations. All the lunch and dinner real world stuff was hard— [I] had to really think."

—High school Algebra II student

Description

The Meal menu (see Figure 1.2) is a menu with a total of at least nine predetermined choices as well as two or more enrichment/optional activities for students. The choices are created at the various levels of Bloom's revised taxonomy and incorporate different learning preferences, with the levels getting progressively higher and more complex as student progress from breakfast to lunch and then dinner. All products carry the same weight for grading and have similar expectations for completion time and effort. The enrichment or optional (dessert) options can be used for extra credit or replace another meal option at the teacher's discretion.

Benefits

Great starter menu. This menu is very straightforward and easy to understand, so time is saved in presenting the completion expectations.

Flexibility. This menu can cover either one topic in depth or three different objectives or aspects within a topic, with each meal representing a different aspect. With this menu, students have the option of completing three products: one from each meal.

Optional enrichment. Although not required, the dessert category of the Meal menu allows students to have the option of going further or deeper if time during the unit permits. This option could also be used, at teacher discretion, as a replacement of low score on one of the meal products.

Chunkability. The Meal menu is very easy to break apart into smaller pieces. Whether you have students who need support in making choices or you only want to focus on one aspect of a topic at a time, this menu can accommodate these decisions. Students could be asked to select a breakfast while the rest of the menu is put on hold until the breakfast product is submitted, then a lunch product is selected, and so on.

Friendly design. Students quickly understand how to use this menu because of its real-world application.

Weighting. All products are equally weighted, so recording grades and maintaining paperwork are easily accomplished with this menu.

Short time period. Meal menus are intended for shorter periods of time, between 1–3 weeks.

Figure 1.2. Meal menu example.

Limitations

No "safety net." Because each product in this menu is recorded as its own grade, it is possible that a student could fail this menu, unless the teacher allows the optional dessert to replace a low grade on one of the meal products.

Time Considerations

Meal menus usually are intended for shorter amounts of completion time—at the most, they should take 3 weeks with students working outside of class and submitting one product each week. If the menu focuses on one topic in-depth and the students have time in class to work on their products, the menu could be completed in one week.

List Menu/"Challenge List"

"Of the different formats I tried this year, I really liked the challenge list format. I could modify the menu simply by changing the [point] goal. When I had a student test out of two days, I simply upped [his or her] goal to 140, and [he or she] worked on [his or her] menu during instructional time. It was a huge success!"

—Secondary math teacher

Description

The basic List menu (see Figure 1.3), or Challenge List, has a total of at least 10 predetermined choices, each with its own point value, and at least one free choice for students. Choices are simply listed with assigned points based on the levels of Bloom's revised taxonomy. The choices carry different weights and have different expectations for completion time and effort. A point criterion is set forth that equals 100%, and students choose how they wish to attain that point goal. There are different versions of the list menu included in this book: the Challenge List (one topic in depth) and a Multitopic List Menu (which, based on its structure, can accommodate more than one topic).

Benefits

Grade-as-you-go. This menu requires that teachers grade products as the students complete them. Actively grading and providing immediate feedback are important so the students can alter their plans and choose to submit additional products to be sure they reach the point goal. Additionally, by grading-as-you-go, teachers will not have piles of products to grade once the menu is completed.

Responsibility. Students have complete control over their grades. Students like the idea that they can guarantee their grade if they complete their required work and meet the expecta-

Figure 1.3. List menu example.

tions outlined in the rubric and product guidelines. If students do not earn full credit on one of the chosen products, they can complete another product to be sure they have met their point goal. This responsibility over their own grades also allows a shift in thinking about grades—whereas many students think of grades in terms of how the teacher judged their work, or what the teacher "gave me," having control over their grades leads students to understand that they earn their grades.

Different learning levels. This menu has the flexibility to allow for individualized contracts for different learning levels within the classroom. Because classrooms may have many ability levels, it might be necessary to contract students based on their ability or results from the pretesting of content. In which case, each student can contract for a certain number of points for his or her 100%.

Concept reinforcement. This menu allows for an in-depth study of the material. With the different levels of Bloom's revised taxonomy being represented, however, students who are at the early stages of learning the concepts can choose lower-level point value products to reinforce the basics before jumping into the higher level activities.

Variety. A list menu offers a larger variety of product choices. There is guaranteed to be a product of interest to everyone. (And if there isn't, there is always free choice!)

Limitations

One topic. If using the traditional challenge list format, this menu can only be used for one topic in depth, so that students cannot miss any specific content.

Cannot guarantee objectives. If the traditional challenge menu is used for more than one topic, it is possible for a student to not have to complete an activity for each objective, depending on the choices he or she makes.

Preparation. Teachers need to have all materials ready at the beginning of the unit for students to be able to choose any of the activities on the list. This expectation requires a degree of advanced planning. (*Note*: This advanced preparation leads to low stress during the unit as all of the materials have already been gathered.)

Time Considerations

List menus usually are intended for shorter amounts of completion time—at the most, 2 weeks. (*Note*: Once you have assembled the materials, the preparation is minimal!)

20-50-80 Menus

As you suggested, I used one of your 20-50-80 menus as homework to review equations of a line the week before we went into solving systems of equations. It was very easy for the students to understand and saved so much time at the beginning of the systems unit. I am going to use these more often.

—Algebra I teacher

Description

A 20-50-80 menu (see Figure 1.4; Magner, 2000), is a variation on a List menu, with a total of at least eight predetermined choices: no more than two choices with a point value of 20, at least four choices with a point value of 50, and at least two choices with a point value of 80. Choices are assigned these points based on the levels of Bloom's revised taxonomy. Choices with a point value of 20 represent the remember and understand levels, choices with a point value of 50 represent the apply and analyze levels, and choices with a point value of 80 represent the evaluate and create levels. All levels of choices carry different weights and have different expectations for completion time and effort. Students are expected to earn 100 points for a 100%. Students choose what combination of products they would like to complete to attain that point goal.

20 Points

❑ _____

❑ _____

50 Points

❑ _____

❑ _____

❑ _____

❑ _____

80 Points

❑ _____

❑ _____

Figure 1.4. 20-50-80 menu example.

Benefits

Responsibility. With this menu, students have complete control over goals and their grade. (*Note*: This is not to say that it is acceptable for students to choose 70% as their goal. The expectation is always that the students will work to achieve or exceed the point goal for the menu.)

Guaranteed activity. This menu's design is set up in such a way that students must complete at least one activity at a higher level of Bloom's revised taxonomy to reach their point goal.

Grade-as-you-go. This menu requires that teachers grade products as the students complete them. Actively grading and providing immediate feedback are important so the students can alter their plans and choose to submit additional products to be sure they reach the point goal. Additionally, by grading-as-you-go, teachers will not have piles of products to grade once the menu is completed.

Low stress. This menu is one of the shortest menus. If students choose well and complete quality products, they could accomplish their goal by completing just two products. This menu is usually not as daunting as some of the longer, more complex menus. The 20-50-80 menu provides students a great introduction into the process of making choices.

Limitations

One topic. If this menu is used for more than one topic, it is possible for a student to not have to complete an activity for each objective, depending on the choices he or she makes. Therefore, a 20-50-80 menu is limited in the number of topics it can assess.

Limited higher level thinking. Students could potentially complete only one activity at a higher level of thinking (although many students will complete more to allow themselves a "cushion" in case they do not earn full credit on a product.

Time Considerations

These menus are usually intended for a shorter amount of completion time—at the most, 2 weeks with students working outside of class, or one week, if class time is allowed for product completion.

Game Show Menu

"It was different, doing a [game show] menu. I had to really consider how I was going to get enough points but still do all the topics. By the time I was done, at least I know I got a 100% on a major grade."

—High school U.S. history student

Description

The Game Show menu (see Figure 1.5) is a complex menu. It can cover multiple topics or objectives with three predetermined choices and a free student choice for each objective. Choices are assigned points based on the levels of Bloom's revised taxonomy. All choices carry different weights and have different expectations for completion time and effort. A point criterion is set forth that equals 100%. Students must complete at least one activity from each objective to reach their goal.

Benefits

Free choice. This menu allows the most free choice options of any of the menu formats. Although it has many choices for students, if they do not want to complete the offered activities, students can propose their activity for each objective addressed on the menu.

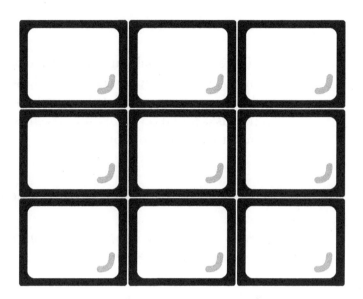

Figure 1.5. Game Show menu example.

Responsibility. This menu allows students to guarantee their grade as long as they meet the point goal for 100%.

Grade-as-you-go. This menu requires that teachers grade products as the students complete them. By grading-as-you-go, teachers will not have piles of products to grade once the menu is completed.

Different learning levels. The game show menu has the flexibility to allow for individualized contracts for different learning levels within the classroom. Each student can create a contract for a certain number of points for his or her 100%.

Objectives guaranteed. The teacher is guaranteed that the students complete an activity from each objective covered, even if it is at a lower level.

Limitations

Confirm expectations. The only real limitation of the Game Show menu is that students (and parents) must understand the guidelines for completing the menu. Teachers need to remember to copy the instruction page on the back of the menu!

Time Considerations

These menus usually are intended to be completed in a longer amount of time. Although teachers could use these menus yearlong (each column could be a grading period), they usually are intended for 2–3 weeks based on the tasks found on the menu as well as the amount of class time allotted for students to work on the menu.

Free Choice

"I try to bring in real-world applications for each concept we cover. Sometimes it might be the students simply answering, 'How does this apply to your life?' So, now I let them use the free choice proposals and they can create something to show me the application of the material."

—High school AP Chemistry teacher

As a menu option, students may be offered the opportunity to submit a free choice for their teacher's consideration. Figure 1.6 shows two sample proposal forms that have been used many times successfully in my classroom. The form provided to students is based on the type of menu being presented. If using a target-based menu like the Tic-Tac-Toe or Meal menu, there is no need to submit a free-choice proposal form that includes the mention of points.

When implementing a menu that includes free choice, a copy of the appropriate free-choice proposal form should be given to each student when the menu is first introduced. The form should be discussed with the students, so they understand the expectations of proposing a free choice. If they do not want to make a proposal after you have discussed the menu and its activities, the students can place unused forms in a designated place. I always had a box of blank proposal forms on the supply table in my classroom, so unused forms could be returned there. Some students may want to keep their free-choice proposal form "just in case"—you may be surprised who wants to submit a proposal form after hearing about the opportunity!

These proposal forms must be submitted before students begin working on their free choice. That way, the teacher knows what the students are working on, and the student knows the expectations for the product

Name: _____ **Teacher's Approval:** _____

Free-Choice Proposal Form for Point-Based Menu

Points Requested:		Points Approved:	

Proposal Outline

1. What specific topic or idea will you learn about?

2. What criteria should be used to grade it? (Neatness, content, creativity, artistic value, etc.)

3. What will your product look like?

4. What materials will you need from the teacher to create this product?

Name: _____ **Teacher's Approval:** _____

Free-Choice Proposal Form for Menus

Proposal Outline

1. What specific topic or idea will you learn about?

2. What criteria should be used to grade it? (Neatness, content, creativity, artistic value, etc.)

3. What will your product look like?

4. What materials will you need from the teacher to create this product?

Figure 1.6. Free-choice proposal forms.

of choice. Once approved, the forms can be stapled to the student's menu sheet for reference. The students can refer to it as they develop their free choice, and when the grading takes place, the teacher can refer to the agreement for the "graded" features of the product.

Each part of the proposal form is important and needs to be discussed with students during the introductory discussion of the form.

- *Name/Teacher's approval.* It is very important that the student submits this form to the teacher. The teacher will carefully review all of the information, give it back to the student for clarification if needed, and then sign the top. Although not always possible, I preferred that the students discuss their forms with me, so we can both be clear about their ideas.
- *Points requested.* Only on the point-based menu proposal form, this is usually where negotiation takes place. Students will often submit their first free-choice request for a very high number of points (even the 100% goal). Students tend to equate the amount of time an activity or product will take with the amount of points it should earn. Unfortunately, the points are always based on the level of Bloom's taxonomy. A PowerPoint with a vocabulary word quiz would get minimal points although it may have taken a long time to create. If the students have not been exposed to the levels of Bloom's taxonomy, the assigning of points can be difficult to explain. Teachers can always refer to the popular "Bloom's Verbs" to help explain the different between time and higher level activities.
- *Points approved.* Only on the point-based menu proposal form, this is the final decision recorded by the teacher once the point haggling is finished.
- *Proposal outline.* This is where the students will tell you everything about the product that they intend to complete. These questions should be completed in such a way that you can picture what they are planning on completing. These questions also show you that the students know what they are planning on completing as well.
  - *What specific topic or idea will you learn about?* Students need to be specific here, not just "science" or "writing." This response is where the students need look at the objectives or standards of the unit and choose which objective they would like to address through their product.

- ○ *What criteria should be used to grade it?* Although there are guidelines for all of the projects that the students might create, it is important for the students to explain what criteria are most important in its evaluation. The student may indicate that the product guideline being used for all of the predetermined product is fine; however, they may also want to add other criteria here.

- ○ *What will your product look like?* It is important that this response be as detailed as possible. If students cannot express what it will "look like," then they have probably not given their free choice enough thought.

- ○ *What materials will you need from the teacher to create this product?* This question is an important consideration. Sometimes students do not have the means to purchase items for their project. These materials can be negotiated as well, but if you ask what students may need, they often will develop even grander ideas for their free choice. This may also be a place for students to note any special equipment or technology needs they may have to create their product.

CHAPTER 2

How to Use Menus in the Classroom

Instructional menus can be used in different ways in the secondary classroom. To decide how to implement your choice menu, the following questions should be considered:

- How confident are your students in making choices and working independently?
- How much intellectually appropriate information is readily available for students to obtain on their own?
- How much prior knowledge of the topic being taught do the students have before the unit or lesson begins?

After considering the responses to these questions, there is a variety of ways to use menus.

 DOI: 10.4324/9781003234357-3

Building Background Knowledge or Accessing Prior Knowledge

"I have students with so many different experiences—sometimes I spend a lot more time than I allotted to review and get everyone up to speed before we get started."

—Secondary social studies teacher

There are many ways to use menus in the classroom. One way that is often overlooked is using menus to review or build background knowledge or access prior knowledge before a unit begins. Using menus this way is beneficial when students have had exposure to upcoming content in the past, perhaps during the previous year's instruction or through life experiences. Many high school students have had preliminary exposure to the basic information needed in their classes. However, students may not remember the details of the content at the depth needed to proceed with the upcoming unit immediately. A shorter menu covering the background or previous year's objectives can be provided the week prior to the new unit. This way, students have the opportunity to recall and engage with the information in a meaningful way, while not using valuable class time during the first day of a new unit to do so. Because the teacher knows that the students have covered the content in the past, the students should be able to work independently on the menu by engaging their prior knowledge. Students work on products from the selected menu as anchor activities and/or homework throughout the week preceding the new unit, with all products being submitted prior to the upcoming unit's initiation. By using menus in this manner, students have been thinking about the upcoming unit for a week and are ready to investigate the topic further. Students are prepared to take their knowledge to a deeper level on the first day of instruction, conserving that much-needed instruction time.

Enrichment and Supplemental Activities

"Just because my students are teenagers doesn't mean they do not need enrichment; the problem is finding time. My curriculum is so packed, and I had always had trouble getting any in. I tried using an enrichment menu for the body systems since I thought we might have enough time. The students really enjoyed it; they seemed to make time for it. I need to use more."

—High school biology teacher

Using menus for enrichment and supplementary activities is the most common way of implementing menus in the classroom. Many teachers who want to "dip their toes" in the menu pool will begin by using menus this way because it does not directly impact their current teaching style. The students usually do not have much background knowledge, and information about the topic may not be readily available to all students while working on the menu.

When using menus for enrichment or supplemental activities, the teacher should introduce the menu and the choice activities at the beginning of a unit—before any instruction has taken place. The teacher then will progress through the content at the normal rate using his or her curricular materials, periodically allowing class and/or homework time throughout the unit for students to work on their menu choices to supplement a deeper understanding of the lessons being taught. Although it may seem counterintuitive to provide enrichment before any instruction takes place, it actually facilitates a need to know, or an epistemic curiosity (Litman, 2005).

This method incorporates an immediate use for the content the teacher is providing. For example, at the beginning of a unit, the teacher introduces the menu with the explanation that students may not have all of the knowledge to complete their choices yet. As instruction progresses, however, more content will be provided, and the students will be prepared to work on new choices. If students want to work ahead, they certainly can find the information on their own, but this is not required. Gifted students often see the ability to work ahead as a challenge and will begin to investigate concepts mentioned in the menu before the teacher has discussed them. Other students may start to develop questions about the concepts and then are ready to ask their questions when the teacher covers the new material. This "advance investigation" helps build an immense pool of background knowledge and potential content questions before the topic is even discussed in the classroom. As teachers, we constantly fight the battle of having students read ahead or "come to class prepared for discussion." By introducing a menu at the beginning of a unit and allowing students to complete products as instruction progresses, we encourage the students to naturally investigate the information and come to class prepared without having to make preparation a separate requirement.

Mainstream Instructional/Flipped Classroom Activities

"On your suggestion, I tried using the Game Show menu with my geometry unit since I had 3 days of instruction that the students knew well and could work on independently. They really responded to the independence."

–Secondary math teacher

Another option for using menus in the classroom is to offer a choice between certain in-class curricular activities. For example, after students have obtained basic instruction outside of the classroom (through research, videos, or other sources), students can be offered a menu of choices to organize their activities and facilitate their learning during class time. The students spend class time working on the activities on their menus; the teacher spends class time facilitating the choices that students have selected.

If teachers follow a more traditional model, menus can be used when students have some limited background knowledge about the content and appropriate information is readily available for them among their classroom resources. The teacher would select which aspects of the content must be directly taught to the students and which could be appropriately learned and reinforced through product menu activities. The unit is then designed using both formal instructional lessons and specific menu days during which the students will use the menu to strengthen the prior knowledge they already have learned, apply the new information, or extend recently presented information in a differentiated way. For this use of menus to be effective, the teacher must feel very comfortable with the students' prior knowledge level and their readiness to work independently.

Mini-Lessons

"I have so many different levels in my classroom, using menus with mini-lessons has been a life saver. I actually can work with small groups and everyone else doesn't run wild!"

—Secondary math teacher

Another option for menu use is the use of mini-lessons, with the menus driving the accompanying classroom activities. This method is best when most of the students have similar degrees of knowledge about the topic. The teacher designs short 10–15-minute mini-lessons, in which students quickly review fundamental concepts that already are familiar to them as well as experience new content in a brief, concise way. After these short mini-lessons, students can select an activity on the menu to demonstrate their understanding of the new concept.

The Game Show menu usually works well with mini-lessons. The menu can be designed so the topics across the top of the menu represent one mini-lesson per day (column). Using menus in this way shortens the amount of time teachers use the guided practice aspect of the lesson, so all instruction and examples should be carefully selected. The benefit of using menus with mini-lessons is the teacher gets to avoid the one-size-fits-all independent practice portion of the lesson. If a few students still struggle after the mini-lesson, they can be pulled into a small group while the other students work on their choices from the menu.

An important consideration when using menus this way is the independence level of the students. For mini-lesson menus to be effective, students will need to be able to work independently for up to 30 minutes after the mini-lesson. Students are often interested in the product they have chosen, so this may not be a critical issue, but it is still one worth mentioning as teachers consider how they would like to use various menus in their classroom.

CHAPTER 3

Guidelines for Products

"It was different being able to do something other than a drawing or folded paper. I haven't made a video for school in years!"

—High school chemistry student

This chapter outlines the different types of products used in the included menus as well as guidelines and expectations for each. It is crucial that students know the expectations of a product before they choose to work on it. By discussing these expectations before the students begin and having the information readily available, you will save frustration on everyone's part.

$1 Contract

"I really appreciate the $1 form. It kept me from having to run to [craft store] and spend $60 on felt and glitter and all of the other things we normally have to buy for projects."

—Parent of one of my students when asked for feedback on a recent menu

 DOI: 10.4324/9781003234357-4

Consideration should be given to the cost of creating the products in any menu. The resources available to students vary within a classroom, and students should not be evaluated on the amount of materials they can purchase to make a product look glittery. The menus in this book are designed to equalize the resources students have available. For most products, the materials are available for under a dollar and can often be found in a teacher's classroom as part of his or her supplies. If a product would require materials from the student, the $1 contract is included as part of the product's guideline. This contract is an important aspect of the explanation of the product. By limiting the amount of money a child can spend, it creates an equality of resources for all students. This limitation also encourages a more creative product. When students are limited by the amount of materials they can readily purchase, they often have to use materials from home in new and unique ways. Figure 3.1 is a sample $1 contract that I have used many times with various products.

The Products

Table 3.1 contains a list of the products used in this book. These products were chosen for their flexibility in meeting learning preferences as well as being popular products most students have experienced and teachers may already use in their classroom. They have been arranged by learning preference—visual, kinesthetic, or auditory.

Each menu has been designed to include products from all of the learning preferences. Some of the products may be listed under more than one area depending on how they are presented or implemented (and some of the best products cross over between areas). The specific expectations (guidelines) for all of the products are presented in an easy-to-read card format that can be reproduced for students. This format is convenient for students to have in front of them when they work on their projects.

Product Frustrations

"One of the biggest reasons I haven't used more than one product at a time is that I have to constantly reexplain what I want for it. Even if the students write it down, it doesn't mean they won't pester me about it all week."

—English I teacher

$1 Contract

I did not spend more than $1.00 on my _____ .

_____   _____

        Student Signature   Date

My child, _____ , did not spend more than $1.00 on the product he or she created.

_____   _____

        Parent Signature   Date

Figure 3.1. $1 contract.

One of the biggest frustrations that accompany the use of a variety of menu products is the barrage of questions about the products themselves. Students can become so engulfed in the products and the criteria for creating them that they do not focus on the content being synthesized. This focus on products is especially true when menus are introduced to students.

Students can spend an exorbitant amount of time asking the teacher about the products mentioned on the menu. When this interrogation begins, what should have been a 10–15-minute menu introduction turns into 45–50 minutes of discussion about product expectations—without any discussion of the content!

During this discussion, teachers may consider showing students examples of the product(s) from the previous year. Although this can be helpful, it can also lead to additional frustration on the part of both the teacher and the students. Some students may not feel that they can produce a product as nice, as big, as special, or as (you fill in the blank) as the example. Alternatively, when shown an example, students might interpret that the teacher would like something exactly like the example he or she showed to students. To avoid this situation, I would propose that when using examples, students are shown a "blank" example that demonstrates how to create the shell of the product. For example, if a window pane is needed, students might be shown a blank piece of paper that the teacher has divided into six panes. The students can then take

Table 3.1
Products

Visual	Kinesthetic	Auditory/Oral
Acrostic	Board Game	Board Game
Advertisement	Book Cover	Children's Book
Book Cover	Bulletin Board Display	Class Game
Brochure/Pamphlet	Card Sort	Classroom Model
Cartoon/Comic Strip	Class Game	Commercial
Children's Book	Classroom Model	Game Show
Choose Your Own	Collage	Interview
Adventure	Commercial	News Report
Collage	Concentration Cards	Play
Crossword Puzzle	Diorama	Presentation of Created
Diary/Journal	Flipbook	Product
Drawing	Folded Quiz Book	PowerPoint–Speaker
E-mail	Game Show	Puppet Show
Folded Quiz Book	Mobile	Speech
Graphic Novel	Model	Song/Rap
Greeting Card	Mural	Student-Taught Lesson
Instruction Card	Museum Exhibit	You Be the Person
Letter	Play	Presentation
Map	Product Cube	Video
Mind Map	Puppet	
Newspaper Article	Quiz Board	
Poster	Scrapbook	
PowerPoint–Stand	Science Experiment	
Alone	Student-Taught Lesson	
Questionnaire	Three-Dimensional	
Quiz	Timeline	
Recipe	Trading Cards	
Scrapbook	Trophy	
Social Media Profile	Video	
Story	WebQuest	
Trading Cards		
Three Facts and a Fib		
Venn Diagram		
WebQuest		
Window Pane		
Worksheet		

the "skeleton" of the product and make it their own as they create their version of the window pane using their information.

Product Guidelines

"Wow. You know how great these are . . . how much time they will save?"

—A group of teachers, when presented with a page of products guidelines for their classroom

Most frustrations associated with the varied products placed on menus can be addressed proactively using standardized, predetermined product guidelines. These guidelines should be shared with students prior to them creating any products. Although these guidelines may look like "mini-rubrics," they are designed in a generic way, such that any time throughout the school year that students select a product, that product's guidelines will apply.

A beneficial side effect of using set guidelines for a product is the security the guideline creates in the choice-making process. Students are often reticent to try something new, as doing so requires taking a risk. Traditionally, when students select products, they ask questions about creating the product, hope they remember all of the details, and submit the product for grading. It can be quite a shock when the students receive the product back and realize that their product was not complete or was not what the teacher expected. As you can imagine, students may not want to take the risk on something new the next time. Instead, they may prefer to stick to what they know and be successful. Using standardized product guidelines, students can begin to feel secure in their choice before they start working on a new product. Without this security, students tend to stay within their comfort zone.

Sharing the Product Guidelines

"Wow! It's already done for us."

—A group of teachers at staff development after
discovering the product guidelines pages

The guidelines for all of the products used on the menus in this book, as well as some potential free-choice options, are included in an easy-to-read card format (see Figure 3.2). Once the topic menu has been selected, there are many ways to share this information with students. There is no one "right way" to share the product guideline information with your students. The method you select depends on your students' abilities and needs.

For students who are independent and responsible (yes, they do exist!), teachers may duplicate and distribute all of the product guidelines pages to students at the beginning of the year. Students can glue them into the front of their notebooks or punch holes and place them in binders. By providing them in advance, each student has his or her copy to use while working on menu products during the school year.

If teachers prefer a more controlled method, class sets can be created. These sets can be created by gluing each product guideline onto a separate index card, hole punching the corner of each card, and placing all of the cards on a metal ring. These ring sets can be put in a central location or at a supply table where students can borrow and return them as they work on their products. Using a ring also allows for the addition of products as they are introduced. Additionally, the rings and index cards can be color-coded based on learning preference, encouraging students to step out of their comfort zone during free choice.

Some teachers prefer to expose students to products as students experience them on their menus. In this case, product guidelines from the menu currently assigned can be enlarged and posted on a bulletin board or wall for easy access during classroom work. Some teachers may choose to reproduce each menu's specific product guidelines on the back of the menu.

No matter which method teachers select to share the product guideline information with the students, teachers will save themselves a lot of time and frustration by having the product guidelines available for student reference (e.g., "Look at your product guidelines—I think that will answer your question").

Acrostic	Advertisement	Board Game
<ul><li>Must be at least 8.5" by 11"</li><li>Must be neatly written or typed</li><li>Target word must be written down the left side of the paper</li><li>Each descriptive phrase chosen must begin with one of the letters from the target word</li><li>Each descriptive phrase chosen must be related to the target word</li><li>Name must be written on the acrostic</li></ul>	<ul><li>Must be at least 8.5" by 11"</li><li>Must include a meaningful slogan</li><li>Must include a color picture of item or service</li><li>Must include price, if appropriate</li><li>Could be developed electronically</li><li>Name must be written on the advertisement</li></ul>	<ul><li>Must have at least four thematic game pieces</li><li>Must have at least 25 colored/thematic squares</li><li>Must have at least 20 question/activity cards</li><li>Must have thematic title on the game</li><li>Must have a complete set of rules for playing the game</li><li>Must be at least the size of an open file folder</li><li>Name must be written on the front of the board game</li></ul>
Book Cover	**Brochure/Pamphlet**	**Bulletin Board Display**
Must include five parts:<ul><li>**Front cover**—title, author, image</li><li>**Cover inside flap**—paragraph summary of the book</li><li>**Back inside flap**—brief biography of author with at least five details</li><li>**Back cover**—editorial comments about book</li><li>**Spine**—title and author<ul><li>» May be placed on actual book, but not necessary</li><li>» Name must be written on the book cover</li></ul></li></ul>	<ul><li>Must be at least 8.5" by 11"</li><li>Must be in three-fold format</li><li>Front fold must have the title and picture</li><li>Must have both pictures and information</li><li>Information must be in paragraph form with at least five facts included</li><li>Bibliography or sources must be provided if needed</li><li>Can be created on computer</li><li>Any pictures from the Internet must have proper credit</li><li>Name must be written on the cover of the brochure</li></ul>	<ul><li>Must fit within assigned space on bulletin board or wall</li><li>Must include at least 10 details</li><li>Must have a title</li><li>Must have at least five different elements (posters, papers, questions, etc.)</li><li>Must have at least one interactive element that engages the reader</li><li>Name must be written on the bottom of the display</li></ul>
Card Sort	**Cartoon/Comic Strip**	**Children's Book**
<ul><li>Must have at least 16 total cards</li><li>Must have at least five cards in each column</li><li>Can have more than two columns if appropriate</li><li>Answer key must be submitted</li><li>All cards must be submitted in a carrying bag</li><li>Name must be written on the carrying bag</li></ul>	<ul><li>Must be at least 8.5" by 11"</li><li>Must have at least six cells</li><li>Must have meaningful dialogue that addresses the task</li><li>Must have color</li><li>Name must be written on the bottom of the cartoon or comic strip</li></ul>	<ul><li>Must have a cover with book's title and student's name as author</li><li>Must have at least 10 pages</li><li>Each page must have an illustration to accompany the story</li><li>Must be neatly written or typed</li><li>Can be developed on the computer</li></ul>

Figure 3.2. Product guidelines.

Choose Your Own Adventure	Class Game	Classroom Model
• Must be neatly written or typed • Can be presented in an electronic format • Reader must be able to transition smoothly between choices • Readers must experience at least four choices in each story "strand" • Must include at least six unique endings • Must be appropriate length to allow for all of the adventures	• Game must allow all class members to participate • Must have only a few, easy-to-understand rules • Must be inventive or a new variation on a current game • Must have multiple question opportunities • Must provide answer key before the game is played • Name must be written on the answer key • The game must be approved by the teacher before being scheduled for play	• Must use everyone in the class in the model • Must not take longer than 2 minutes to arrange everyone • Students must be able to understand the part they play in the model • After the model is created, the explanation of the model must not take longer than 2 minutes • Must submit a paragraph that shares how the arrangement of students represents the concept being modeled • Name must be written on the paragraph submitted
Collage	**Commercial/Infomercial**	**Concentration Cards**
• Must be at least 8.5" by 11" • Pictures must be neatly cut from magazines or newspapers (no clip art) • Must label items as required in task • Name must be written on the bottom of the collage	• Must be between 1 and 3 minutes • Script must be turned in before commercial is presented • May be either live or recorded beforehand based on teacher discretion • Must have props or some form of costume(s) • Can include more than one person • Name must be written on the script	• Must have at least 20 index cards (10 matching sets) • Can use both pictures and words • Information must be placed on just one side of each card • Must include an answer key that shows the matches • All cards must be submitted in a carrying bag • Name must be written on the carrying bag
Cross Cut Model/Diagram	**Crossword Puzzle**	**Diary/Journal**
• Must include a scale to show the relationship between product and the actual item • Must include details about each layer • If creating a model, must also meet the criteria of a model • If creating a diagram, must also meet the criteria of a poster • Name must be written on the model	• Must have at least 20 significant words or phrases included • Clues must be appropriate • Must include puzzle and answer key • Can be created using a computer • Name must be written on the crossword puzzle	• Must be neatly written or typed • Must include the appropriate number of entries • Must include a date for each entry if appropriate • Must be written in first person • Name must be written on the diary or journal

Figure 3.2. Continued.

   © Taylor & Francis • *Differentiating Instruction With Menus: Chemistry* • Grades 9–12

Diorama	Drawing	E-mail
• Must be at least 4" by 5" by 8" • Must be self-standing • All interior space must be covered with relevant pictures and information • Name must be written on the back in permanent ink • Must submit a signed $1 contract • Informational/title card must be attached to diorama	• Must be at least 8.5" by 11" • Must show what is requested in the task statement • Must include color • Must be neatly drawn by hand • Must have title • Name must be written on the back	• Must be neatly written or typed • Must cover the specific topic of the task • Must include standard to, from, and subject • Must include appropriate (but fictitious) e-mail addresses of sender and recipient • Must be signed with custom signature from sender
Essay	**Flipbook**	**Folded Quiz Book**
• Must be neatly written or typed • Must cover the specific topic in detail • Must be at least three paragraphs • Must include bibliography or sources if appropriate • Name must be written in the heading of the essay	• Must be at least 8.5" by 11" folded in half • All information or opinions must be supported by facts • Must be created with the correct number of flaps cut into the top • Color is optional • Name must be written on the back of the flipbook	• Must be at least 8.5" by 11" • Must have at least 10 questions • Must be created with the correct number of flaps cut into the top • Questions must be written or typed neatly on upper flaps • Answers must be written or typed neatly inside each flap • Color is optional • Name must be written on the back of the quiz book
Game Show	**Greeting Card**	**Instruction Card**
• Must have an emcee or host • Must have at least two contestants • Must have at least one regular round and a bonus round • Questions must be content specific • Props can be used, but are not mandatory • Name must be written on the questions used in the game	**Must include four parts:** • **Front**—colored pictures, words optional • **Front inside**—personal note related to topic • **Back inside**—greeting or saying, must meet menu task • **Back outside**—logo, publisher, and price for card » Name must be written on the back of the card	• Must be no larger than 5" by 8" • Must be created on heavy paper or card • Must be neatly written or typed • Must use color drawings • Must provide instructions stated in the task • Name must be written on the back of the card

Figure 3.2. Continued.

Interview	Letter	Map
• Must have at least eight questions important to the topic being studied • Person chosen for interview must be an "expert" and qualified to provide answers based on product criteria • Questions and answers must be neatly written or typed • Name must be written on the interview questions	• Must be neatly written or typed • Must use proper letter format • Must have at least three paragraphs • Must follow type of letter stated in the menu (friendly, persuasive, informational) • Name must be included in the letter in a meaningful way	• Must be at least 8.5" by 11" • Must contain accurate information • Must include at least 10 relevant locations • Must include compass rose, legend, scale, key • Name must be written on the back of the map

Mind Map	Mobile	Model
• Must be at least 8.5" by 11" • Must use unlined paper • Must have one central idea • Must follow the "no more than four rule": There must be no more than four words coming from any one word • Must be neatly written or developed using a computer program • Name must be written on the mind map	• Must contain at least 10 pieces of related information • Must include color and pictures • Must include at least three layers of hanging information • Must be able to hang in a balanced way • Name must be written on one of the cards hanging from the mobile	• Must be at least 8" by 8" by 12" • Parts of model must be labeled • Must be in scale when appropriate • Must include a title card • Name must be permanently written on model

Mural	Museum Exhibit	News Report
• Must be at least 22" x 54" • Must have at least five pieces of important information • Must have colored pictures • Words are optional, but must have title • Name must be written on the back of the mural in a permanent way	• Must have title for exhibit • Must include at least five "artifacts" • Each artifact must be labeled with a neatly written card • Exhibit must fit within the size assigned • Must submit a signed $1 contract • No expensive or irreplaceable objects may be used in the display • Name must be written on a label card in the exhibit	• Must address the who, what, where, when, why, and how of the topic • Script of news report must be turned in with product, or before if performance will be "live" • May be either live or recorded beforehand based on teacher discretion • Name announced during the performance and clearly written on script

Figure 3.2. Continued.

Newspaper Article	Play/Skit	Poster
• Must be informational in nature • Must follow standard newspaper format • Must include picture with caption that supports article • Must contain at least three paragraphs • Must be neatly written or typed • Name must be written at the top of the article	• Must be between 3 and 5 minutes • Script must be turned in before play is presented • May be presented to an audience or recorded for future showing to audience based on teacher discretion • Must have props or some form of costume • Can include more than one person • Name must be written on the script that is submitted with the play	• Must be the size of a standard poster board • Must contain at least five pieces of important information • Must have title • Must have both words and pictures • Name must be written on the back of the poster in a permanent way • Bibliography or sources must be included as needed

PowerPoint–Stand Alone	PowerPoint–Speaker	Project Cube
• Must contain at least 10 informational slides • Must not have more than 10 words per page • Slides must have color and no more than one graphic per page • Animations are optional but must not distract from the information being presented • Bibliography or sources must be included as needed • Name must be written on the first slide of the PowerPoint	• Must contain at least 10 informational slides • Must not have more than two words per page • Slides must have color and no more than one graphic per page • Animations are optional but must not distract from information being presented • Presentation must be timed and flow with the speech being given • Name must be written on the first slide of the PowerPoint	• All six sides of the cube must be filled with information as stated in the task • Must be neatly written or typed • Name must be printed neatly on the bottom of one of the sides of the cube • Must be submitted flat for grading

Puppet	Questionnaire	Quiz
• Puppet must be handmade and must have a movable mouth • A list of supplies used to make the puppet must be turned in with the puppet • Must submit a signed $1 contract • If used in a puppet show, all play criteria must be met as well • Name must be written on the inside of the puppet where it can be seen	• Must be neatly written or typed • Must contain at least 10 questions with possible answers • Must contain at least one answer that requires a written response • Questions must be helpful to gathering information on the topic begin studied • If questionnaire is to be used, at least 15 people must provide answers • Name must be written at the top of the questionnaire	• Must be at least a half sheet of paper • Must be neatly written or typed • Must cover the specific topic in detail • Must include at least five questions, including at least one short answer question • Must have at least one graphic • An answer key must be turned in with the quiz • Name must be written on the top of the quiz

Figure 3.2. Continued.

Quiz Board	Recipe/Recipe Card	Scrapbook
• Must have at least five questions • Must have at least five answers, although there could be more for distractors • Must use a system with lights to facilitate self-checking • Name must be written in a permanent way on the back of the quiz board	• Must be written neatly or typed on a piece of paper or an index card • Must have a list of ingredients with measurements for each • Must have numbered steps that explain how to make the recipe • Name must be written at the top of the recipe card	• Cover of scrapbook must have a meaningful title and student's name • Must have at least five themed pages • Each page must have at least one meaningful picture • All photos and pictures must have captions • Bibliography or sources must be included as needed
Social Media Profile	**Song/Rap**	**Speech**
• Must include profile picture • Must include other relevant information about the "person" • Must include at least five status updates with comments from "friends" • Can be created electronically or in poster format • Name must be included on the social media profile in a creative way	• Must be original (not found online or sung by anyone else before) • Words or lyrics must make sense • May be either live or recorded beforehand based on teacher discretion • Written words must be turned in before performance or with taped song • Must be at least 2 minutes in length • Name must be written on the written words submitted with the song or rap	• Must be at least 2 minutes in length • Must not be read from written paper • Note cards can be used • Written speech must be turned in before speech is presented • May be either live or recorded beforehand based on teacher discretion • Voice must be clear, loud, and easy to understand • Name must be written on the written speech
Story	**Three-Dimensional Timeline**	**Three Facts and a Fib**
• Must be neatly written or typed • Must have all elements of a well-written story (setting, characters, conflict, rising action, and resolution) • Must be appropriate length to allow for story elements • Name must be written on the story	• Must not be bigger than a standard-size poster board • Must be divided into equal time units • Must contain at least 10 important dates • Must have at least two sentences explaining why each date is important • Must have an meaningful object securely attached beside each date to represent that date • Objects must be creative • Must be able to explain how each object represents each date or event • Name must be written at the bottom of the timeline	• Can be handwritten, typed, or created in PowerPoint • Must include exactly four statements: three true statements (facts) and one false statement (fib) • False statement must not be obvious • Brief paragraph must accompany product that explains why the fib is false • Name must be written on the product

Figure 3.2. Continued.

Trading Cards	Trophy	Venn Diagram
• Must include at least 10 cards • Each card must be at least 3" by 5" • Each card must have a colored picture • Must contain at least three facts on the subject of the card • Cards must have information on both sides • All cards must be submitted in a carrying bag • Name must be written on the carrying bag	• Must be at least 6" tall • Must have a base with the name of the person getting the trophy and the name of the award written neatly or typed on it • Top of trophy must be appropriate and represent the nature of the award • Name must be written on the bottom of the award • Must be an original trophy (avoid reusing a trophy from home)	• Must be at least 8.5" by 11" • Diagram shapes must be thematic (rather than just circles) and neatly drawn • Must have a title for entire diagram and a title for each section • Must have at least six items in each section of the diagram • Name must be written neatly on the back of the paper

Video	WebQuest	Window Pane
• Must use video format • Must submit a written plan or story board with project • Students must arrange their own way to record their video or allow teacher **at least** 3 days notice for help in obtaining a way to record the video • Must cover pertinent information • Name must be written on the label or in the file name	• Must quest through at least five high-quality websites • Websites must be linked in the document • Can be submitted using a word processor or PowerPoint • Must contain at least three questions for each website • Must address the topic • Name must be written on the WebQuest or in the file name	• Must be at least 8.5" by 11" on unlined paper • Must contain at least six squares • Each square must include both a picture and words • All pictures must be both creative and meaningful • Must be neatly written or typed • Name must be written on the bottom right hand corner of the front of the window pane

Worksheet	You Be the Person Presentation	
• Must be 8.5" by 11" • Must be neatly written or typed • Must cover the specific topic or question in detail • Must be creative in design • Must have at least one graphic • An answer key must be turned in with the worksheet • Name must be written at the top of the worksheet	• Presenter must take on the role of the person • Must cover at least five important facts about the life or achievements of the person • Must be between 2 and 4 minutes in length • Script must be turned in before information is presented • Must be presented to an audience with the ability to answer questions while in character • Must have props or some form of costume • Name must be written on the script	

Figure 3.2. Continued.

CHAPTER 4

Rubrics

"One rubric—and I can grade everything? Now we are talking!"

—Group of secondary teachers

The most common reason teachers feel uncomfortable with menus is the need for fair and equal grading. If all of the students create the same product, teachers feel these products are easier to grade than 100 different products, none of which looks like any other. The great equalizer for hundreds of different products is a generic rubric that can evaluate the important qualities of an excellent product.

All-Purpose Rubric

Figure 4.1 is an example of a rubric that has been classroom tested with various menus. This rubric can be used with any point value activity presented in a menu, as there are five criteria, and the columns represent full points, half points, and no points. For example, if a student completes a 20-point product, each criterion would be worth four points (full

 DOI: 10.4324/9781003234357-5

All-Purpose Rubric

Name: _____

Criteria	Excellent (Full Credit)	Good (Half Credit)	Poor (No Credit)	Self
Content Is the content of the product well chosen?	Content chosen represents the best choice for the product. Information or graphics are well chosen and related to content.	Information or graphics are related to content, but are not the best choice for the product.	Information or graphics present do not appear related to the topic or task.	
Completeness Is everything included in the product?	All information needed is included. Product meets the product guideline criteria and the criteria of the menu task.	Some important information is missing. Product meets the product guideline criteria and the criteria of the menu task.	Most important information is missing. The product does not meet the task or does not meet the product criteria.	
Creativity Is the product original?	Presentation of information is from a new and original perspective. Graphics are original. Product includes elements of fun and interest.	Presentation of information is from a new perspective. Graphics are not original. Product has elements of fun and interest.	There is no evidence of new thoughts or perspectives in the product, or any part of the product was plagiarized.	
Correctness Is all of the information included correct?	All information presented is correct and accurate.		Any portion of the information presented in product is incorrect.	
Communication Is the information in the product well communicated?	All information is neat and easy to read. Product is in appropriate format and shows significant effort. Oral presentation was easy to understand and presented with fluency.	Most (80%) of the product is neat and easy to read. Product is in appropriate format and shows significant effort. Oral presentation was easy to understand, with some fluency.	More than 20% of the product is not neat and easy to read, or the product is not in the appropriate format. It does not show significant effort. Oral presentation was not fluent or easy to understand.	
			Total Grade:	

Figure 4.1. All-purpose rubric.

points), two points (half points) and zero (no points). Although Tic-Tac-Toe and Meal menus are not point based, this rubric can also be used to grade products from these menus. Teachers simply assign 100 points to each of the three products on the Tic-Tac-Toe and Meal menus. Then each criterion would be worth 20 points, and the all-purpose rubric can be used to grade each product individually.

There are different ways that teachers can share this rubric with students. Some teachers prefer to provide it when they present a menu to students. The rubric can be reproduced on the back of the menu along with its guidelines. The rubric can also be given to students at the beginning of the year with the product guideline cards. This way, students will always know the expectations as they complete projects throughout the school year. Some teachers prefer to keep a master copy of the rubric for themselves and post an enlarged copy on a bulletin board. If teachers wanted to share the rubric with parents, they could provide a copy for parents during back-to-school night, open house, or on private teacher web pages so that the parents will understand how teachers will grade their children's products.

No matter how teachers choose to share the rubric with students, the first time students see this rubric, it should be explained in detail, especially the last column, titled "Self." It is imperative that students self-evaluate their products. The Self column can provide a unique perspective on the product as it is being graded. *Note*: This rubric was designed to be specific enough that students will understand the criteria the teacher is seeking, but general enough that they can still be as creative as they like in the creation of their product.

Science Experiment Rubrics and Student-Taught Lessons

Although the all-purpose rubric can be used for all of the activities included on the menus in this book, there are two occasions that seem to warrant a special rubric: science experiments and student-taught lessons. These are unique situations, with many fine details that must be considered to create a quality product.

As high schoolers, most students understand the scientific method and many are ready to begin their own investigations. Understanding the scientific method, however, does not always guarantee that students know how to apply it to their own investigations. The student-created experiment rubric (see Figure 4.2) will guide students as they develop their experiences.

Student-taught lessons are another unique situation. School curricula are already packed with information, and teachers often feel that turning class time over to students should only be done if the experience will benefit everyone involved. Teachers would like to allow students to teach their classmates but are concerned about quality lessons and may not be comfortable with the grading aspect of the assignment. Rarely do students understand all of the components that go into designing an effective lesson. The student-taught lesson rubric (see Figure 4.3) helps focus students on the important aspects of a well-designed lesson and allows teachers to make the evaluation a little more subjective.

Student-Created Experiment Rubric

Name: _____

Criteria	Excellent	Good	Fair	Poor	Self
Title	5	3	1	0	
The title is appropriate; represents lab.	Title is appropriate, unique, and represents lab.	Title is present and appropriate, but not unique.	Title is present, but there is no significance to this lab.	Not present.	
Problem/Purpose	5	3	1	0	
Problem stated as question; appropriate for lab. Purpose stated as sentence.	Problem/purpose is present and contains proper punctuation and format.	Problem/purpose is present and contains proper punctuation, but not in proper format.	Problem/purpose is present, but does not contain proper format or punctuation.	Not present.	
Hypothesis	10	5	3	0	
Stated as an if/then statement (if appropriate) and relates to the problem.	Hypothesis is present, contains proper punctuation and format, and relates to the problem.	Hypothesis is present, contains proper punctuation, and relates to the problem, but not in proper format.	Hypothesis is present, but no obvious relation to problem. It contains proper punctuation, but not in proper format.	Not present or does not relate to problem.	
Materials	10	5	3	0	
All materials present and all exact in description (e.g., "250 ml beaker" rather than "beaker").	All materials present and all exact in description.	Missing no more than one item, and all exact descriptions.	Missing no more than one item, and 90% of the descriptions are exact.	Missing no more than one item, but less than 90% of the descriptions are exact, or materials are not present.	
Procedure	20	15	8	0	
Procedure is sequential and easy to read. Exact; written in a way that would allow others to repeat the experiment.	The procedure is sequential, easy to read, and contains proper punctuation. The procedure is exact.	The procedure is sequential and easy to read, but missing some proper punctuation. The procedure is exact.	The procedure is not sequential, not easy to read, or missing some proper punctuation, but is exact.	The procedure is not exact, not easy to read, not sequential, or not present.	

Figure 4.2. Student-created experiment rubric.

Student-Created Experiment Rubric
Continued

Criteria	Excellent	Good	Fair	Poor	Self
	15	10	5	0	
Data Table	Data are recorded in an appropriate manner, easy to read and understand, and have proper units, titles, and descriptions.	Data table has no title, but is easy to read, all numbers are entered with units, and columns and rows are labeled.	Data table has no title, but is easy to read, no more than three numbers are entered without units, and columns and rows are labeled.	Data table has no title, is not easy to read, some numbers are entered without units, columns and rows are not labeled, or not present.	
	15	10	5	0	
Representation of Data	Data are recorded in an appropriate manner, and are easy to read and understand. Graph has proper units, titles, and descriptions, and the proper graph has been chosen.	Data are easy to read; graph has units and descriptors, but no title; and variables are on the correct axis. Data are clearly represented.	Data are easy to read; graph has descriptors, but no units or title; and variables are on the correct axis. Data are clearly represented.	Data are easy to read, graph has missing descriptors, variables are on the incorrect axis, or not present.	
	20	12	4	0	
Conclusion	Conclusion is in paragraph form, revisits hypothesis, explains how the lab was conducted, suggests margins for error, and makes a new hypothesis if needed.	Contains proper punctuation and form, describes experiment, revisits hypothesis, and suggests a new one if necessary, but does not describe points of error.	Missing proper punctuation or form, or revisits hypothesis but does not suggest a new one if necessary.	Does not revisit hypothesis or conclusion is not present.	
				Total Grade:	

Figure 4.2. Continued.

Student-Taught Lesson Rubric   Name: _____

Parts of Lesson	Excellent	Good	Fair	Poor	Self
Prepared and Ready All materials and lesson ready at the start of class period, from warm-up to conclusion of lesson.	**10** Everything is ready to present.	**6** Lesson is present, but small amount of scrambling.	**3** Lesson is present, but major scrambling.	**0** No lesson ready or missing major components.	
Understanding Presenter(s) understands the material well. Students understand information presented.	**20** All information is correct and in correct format.	**12** Presenter understands; 25% of students do not.	**4** Presenter understands; 50% of students do not.	**0** Presenter is confused.	
Complete Includes all significant information from section or topic.	**15** Includes all important information.	**10** Includes most important information.	**2** Includes less than 50% of the important information.	**0** Information is not related.	
Practice Includes some way for students to practice the information presented.	**20** Practice present; was well chosen.	**10** Practice present; can be applied effectively.	**5** Practice present; not related or best choice.	**0** No practice or students are confused.	
Interest/Fun Most of the class was involved, interested, and participating.	**15** Everyone interested and participating.	**10** 75% actively participating.	**5** Less than 50% actively participating.	**0** Everyone off task.	
Creativity Information presented in an imaginative way.	**20** Wow, creative! I never would have thought of that!	**12** Good ideas!	**5** Some good pieces but general instruction.	**0** No creativity; all lecture, notes, or worksheet.	

Your Topic/Objective:

Comments:

Don't forget: All copy requests and material requests must be made at least 24 hours in advance.

Figure 4.3. Student-taught lesson rubric.

PART II

The Menus

How to Use the Menu Pages

Each menu in this section has:
- an introduction page for the teacher that includes the answers to any calculations included on the menu,
- the content menu, and
- any specific activities mentioned in the menu.

Introduction Pages

The introduction pages are meant to provide an overview of each menu. They are divided into five areas.

- *Objectives Covered Through the Menu and Activities.* This area will list all of the instructional objectives that the menu can address. Although all of the objectives integrated into the menus correlate to state and national standards, these targets will be stated in a generic, teacher-friendly way. Menus are arranged in such a way that if students complete the guidelines outlined in the instructions for the menu, all of these objectives will be covered.

 DOI: 10.4324/9781003234357-6

- *Materials Needed by Students for Completion.* For each menu, it is expected that the teacher will provide, or students will have access to, the following materials:
  - lined paper,
  - blank 8.5" by 11" white paper,
  - glue, and
  - colored pencils or markers.

  The introduction page also includes a list of additional materials that may be needed by students as they complete the menu. Students do have the choice of the menu items they can complete, so it is possible that the teacher will not need all of these materials for every student.

- *Special Notes on the Use of This Menu.* Some menus allow students to choose to present products to their classmates, build items out of recycled materials, or build quiz boards. This section will outline any special tips on managing products that may require more time, supplies, or space. This section will also share any tips to consider for a particular activity.

- *Time Frame.* Each menu has its ideal time frame based on its structure, but all need at least one week to complete. Menus that assess more objectives are better suited to more than 2 weeks. This section will give you an overview of the best time frame for completing the entire menu, as well as options for shorter time periods. If teachers do not have time to devote to a whole menu, they certainly can choose the 1–2-day option for any menu topic students are currently studying.

- *Suggested Forms.* This section contains a list of the rubrics or forms that should be available for students as the menus are introduced. If a menu has a free-choice option, the appropriate proposal form also will be listed here.

CHAPTER 5

Process Skills

DOI: 10.4324/9781003234357-7

20 Points
☐ _____
☐ _____
50 Points
☐ _____
☐ _____
☐ _____
☐ _____
80 Points
☐ _____
☐ _____

Metric Conversions

20-50-80 Menu

Objectives Covered Through This Menu and These Activities

- Students will practice converting between different metric measurements.
- Students will express and manipulate chemical quantities using chemical conventions and mathematical procedures.
- Students will communicate valid conclusions supported by data.

Materials Needed by Students for Completion

- Method for recording responses to word problems on the menu

Special Notes on the Use of This Menu

- This menu is a problem menu; it asks students to demonstrate their knowledge and answer one or more higher level word problems. It is set up in such a way that students will have to complete at least one of the word problems. When introducing this menu, teachers will need to have already determined how they would like these problems completed and recorded for grading. Remember, this is the opportunity to hold high standards when it comes to showing work and defending answers!

Time Frame

- 1–2 weeks—Students are given a menu as the unit is started, and the teacher discusses all of the options on the menu. As the different options are discussed, students will choose the problems they are most interested in completing so that they meet their goal of 100 points. As the lessons progress through the week(s), the teacher and students refer back to the menu options associated with the content being taught.
- 1–2 days—The teacher chooses a problem from the menu to use with the entire class.

Suggested Forms

- All-purpose rubric
- Proposal form for point-based projects

Answers to Menu Problems

Problem 1: An Olympic triathlon requires athletes to swim for 1,500 m, bike for 40 km, and run for 10 km. How many total centimeters are required in this competition?

$$Swim: 1{,}500 \text{ m} \cdot \frac{100 \text{ cm}}{1 \text{ m}} = 150{,}000 \text{ cm}$$

$$Bike: 40 \text{ km} \cdot \frac{1{,}000 \text{ m}}{1 \text{ km}} \cdot \frac{100 \text{ cm}}{1 \text{ m}} = 4{,}000{,}000 \text{ cm}$$

$$Run: 10 \text{ km} \cdot \frac{1{,}000 \text{ m}}{1 \text{ km}} \cdot \frac{100 \text{ cm}}{1 \text{ m}} = 1{,}000{,}000 \text{ cm}$$

$$\text{Swim} + \text{Bike} + \text{Run} = 5{,}150{,}000 \text{ cm or } 5.15 \times 10^6 \text{ cm}$$

Problem 2: You have built a bridge for a science competition, and it needs to hold at least 10 kg. You know that a penny weighs 2.5 g, a nickel weighs 5 g, and a quarter weighs 5.67 g. If you can only use one type of coin, how many of each coin would you need to test your bridge?

$$Penny: 10 \text{ kg} \cdot \frac{1{,}000 \text{ g}}{1 \text{ kg}} = \frac{10{,}000 \text{ g}}{2.5 \text{ g per penny}} = 4{,}000 \text{ pennies}$$

$$Nickel: 10 \text{ kg} \cdot \frac{1{,}000 \text{ g}}{1 \text{ kg}} = \frac{10{,}000 \text{ g}}{5 \text{ g per nickel}} = 2{,}000 \text{ nickels}$$

$$Quarter: 10 \text{ kg} \cdot \frac{1{,}000 \text{ g}}{1 \text{ kg}} = \frac{10{,}000 \text{ g}}{5.67 \text{ g per quarter}} = 1{,}764 \text{ quarters}$$

Problem 3: A standard swimming pool holds about 375 kL of water. If a teacup holds about 150 mL, how many teacups of water would it take to fill a swimming pool?

$$375 \text{ kL} \cdot \frac{1{,}000 \text{ L}}{1 \text{ kL}} \cdot \frac{1{,}000 \text{ mL}}{1 \text{ L}} = \frac{375{,}000{,}000 \text{ mL}}{150 \text{ mL per teacup}} = 2{,}500{,}000 \text{ teacups}$$

$$\text{or } 2.5 \times 10^6 \text{ teacups}$$

Problem 4: In 2017, a Virginia man paid sales tax on his two cars, a total of \$2,987.14 in pennies. Considering that a penny weighs 2.5 g, how heavy was his payment in kilograms?

$$\$2{,}987.14 \cdot \frac{100 \text{ pennies}}{1 \text{ dollar}} \cdot \frac{2.5 \text{ g}}{1 \text{ penny}} \cdot \frac{1 \text{ kg}}{1{,}000 \text{ g}} = 746.79 \text{ kg or } 747 \text{ kg}$$

Problem 5: The average stride of a squirrel is 32 cm. If a squirrel can travel up to 3.6 km on a daily basis, approximately how many strides does it take in a day?

$$3.6 \text{ km} \cdot \frac{1{,}000 \text{ m}}{1 \text{ km}} \cdot \frac{100 \text{ cm}}{1 \text{ m}} = \frac{360{,}000 \text{ cm}}{32 \text{ cm per stride}} = 11{,}250 \text{ strides}$$

Problem 6: An average garden snail moves at a rate of 1 mm/sec. How fast would this be in kilometers per hour?

$$\frac{1 \text{ mm}}{\text{sec}} \cdot \frac{1 \text{ m}}{1{,}000 \text{ mm}} \cdot \frac{1 \text{ km}}{1{,}000 \text{ m}} \cdot \frac{60 \text{ sec}}{1 \text{ min}} \cdot \frac{60 \text{ min}}{1 \text{ hr}}$$

$$= .0036 \text{ km/hr or } 3.60 \times 10^{-3} \text{ km/hr}$$

Problem 7: A chocolate bar weighs 43 g. If 55.8% of the chocolate bar is sugar, and the company can make approximately 31,536,000 chocolate bars, running its factories 24 hours straight every day of the year, how many kilograms of sugar does the company use each hour?

$$43 \text{ g} \cdot \frac{55.8 \text{ g sugar}}{100 \text{ g bar}} \cdot \frac{1 \text{ kg sugar}}{1000 \text{ g sugar}} = .024 \text{ kg sugar per bar}$$

$$\text{or } 2.4 \times 10^{-2} \text{ kg sugar per bar}$$

$$\frac{31{,}536{,}000 \text{ bars}}{1 \text{ year}} \cdot \frac{1 \text{ year}}{365 \text{ days}} \cdot \frac{1 \text{ day}}{24 \text{ hours}} \cdot \frac{.024 \text{ kg sugar}}{\text{bar}}$$

$$= 86.4 \text{ kg of sugar per hour}$$

Metric Conversions

Directions: Choose at least two activities from the menu below. The activities must total 100 points. Place a checkmark next to each box to show which activities you will complete. All activities must be completed by _____ .

---

20 Points

❑ **Problem 1:** An Olympic triathlon requires athletes to swim for 1,500 m, bike for 40 km, and run for 10 km. How many total centimeters are required in this competition?

❑ **Problem 2:** You have built a bridge for a science competition, and it needs to hold at least 10 kg. You know that a penny weighs 2.5 g, a nickel weighs 5 g, and a quarter weighs 5.67 g. If you can only use one type of coin, how many of each coin would you need to test your bridge?

---

50 Points

❑ **Problem 3:** A standard swimming pool holds about 375 kL of water. If a teacup holds about 150 mL, how many teacups of water would it take to fill a swimming pool?

❑ **Problem 4:** In 2017, a Virginia man paid sales tax on his two cars, a total of $2,987.14 in pennies. Considering that a penny weighs 2.5 g, how heavy was his payment in kilograms?

❑ **Problem 5:** The average stride of a squirrel is 32 cm. If a squirrel can travel up to 3.6 km on a daily basis, approximately how many strides does it take in a day?

❑ **Free choice on metric conversion problems**—Prepare a proposal form and submit it to your teacher for approval.

---

80 Points

❑ **Problem 6:** An average garden snail moves at a rate of 1 mm/sec. How fast would this be in kilometers per hour?

❑ **Problem 7:** A chocolate bar weighs 43 g. If 55.8% of the chocolate bar is sugar, and the company can make approximately 31,536,000 chocolate bars, running its factories 24 hours straight every day of the year, how many kilograms of sugar does the company use each hour?

```
20 Points
□ _____
□ _____
50 Points
□ _____
□ _____
□ _____
□ _____
80 Points
□ _____
□ _____
```

Significant Figures

20-50-80 Menu

Objectives Covered Through This Menu and These Activities

- Students will be able to explain and calculate significant figures accurately.
- Students will be able to state the importance of significant figures when completing calculations.
- Students will critique scientific explanations and evaluate the impact of research on scientific thought.

Materials Needed by Students for Completion

- Poster board or large white paper
- Blank index cards (for trading cards)
- Large blank lined index cards (for instruction cards)
- Holiday lights (for quiz boards)
- Aluminum foil (for quiz boards)
- Wires (for quiz boards)

Special Notes on the Use of This Menu

- This menu gives students the opportunity to teach a concept. This can take a significant amount of time and organization. It can save time if the students who choose to do a lesson can sign up for a designated day and time that is determined when the menu is distributed.
- This menu provides the opportunity for students to create a quiz board. There are many variations for these quiz boards. Instructional videos and written instructions are readily available online.

Time Frame

- 1–2 weeks—Students are given a menu as the unit is started, and the teacher discusses all of the product options on the menu. As the different options are discussed, students will choose the activities they are most interested in completing so that they meet their goal of 100 points. As the lessons progress through the week(s), the teacher and students refer back to the menu options associated with the content being taught.

- 1–2 days—The teacher chooses an activity or product from the menu to use with the entire class.

Suggested Forms

- All-purpose rubric
- Student-taught lesson rubric
- Proposal form for point-based projects

Significant Figures

Directions: Choose at least two activities from the menu below. The activities must total 100 points. Place a checkmark next to each box to show which activities you will complete. All activities must be completed by _____ .

---

20 Points

☐ Write an instruction card that tells the steps needed to determine the significant figures of a measurement.

☐ Make a set of trading cards for 1–5 significant figures. Your cards should include a variety of examples that include zeros.

---

50 Points

☐ Write and perform an original song that could be used to help others understand how to give answers to word problems using the correct number of significant figures. Your song should include at least one example.

☐ Build a quiz board that requires matching chemistry-based word problems to answers with the correct number of significant figures. Each problem and answer should include at least one zero. Be tricky!

☐ Write Three Facts and a Fib about the common mistakes people make when determining the significant figures of a number.

☐ **Free choice on using significant figures**—Prepare a proposal form and submit it to your teacher for approval.

---

80 Points

☐ Prepare a student-taught lesson on significant figures. Your lesson should include examples, how to calculate significant figures, and why they are important in chemistry calculations.

☐ Investigate the importance of accurate significant figures on research in the sciences. Write an essay that shares at least one occasion when a mistake in significant figures impacted a research project.

Accuracy and Precision

20-50-80 Menu

Objectives Covered Through This Menu and These Activities

- Students will be able to distinguish between accuracy and precision as it applies in chemistry as well as real life.
- Students will critique scientific explanations and evaluate the impact of research on scientific thought.

Materials Needed by Students for Completion

- Poster board or large white paper
- Recording software or application (for news reports)
- Microsoft PowerPoint or other slideshow software
- Scrapbooking materials
- Recycled materials (for museum exhibits)

Special Notes on the Use of This Menu

- This menu gives students the opportunity to create a news report. The grading and sharing of these products can often be facilitated by having students prerecord their product using whatever technology is most convenient for the teacher. This allows the teacher to decide when it will be shown as well as keeps the presentation to its intended length. If recording options are limited, this activity can be modified by allowing students to act out the product (like a play) in front of the class.
- This menu asks students to use recycled materials to create their museum exhibit. This does not mean only plastic and paper; instead, students should focus on using materials in new ways. It works well if a box is started for "recycled" contributions at the beginning of the school year. That way, students always have access to these types of materials.

Time Frame

- 1–2 weeks—Students are given a menu as the unit is started, and the teacher discusses all of the product options on the menu. As the different options are discussed, students will choose the activities they are most interested in completing so that they meet their goal of 100

points. As the lessons progress through the week(s), the teacher and students refer back to the menu options associated with the content being taught.
- 1–2 days—The teacher chooses an activity or product from the menu to use with the entire class.

Suggested Forms
- All-purpose rubric
- Proposal form for point-based projects

Accuracy and Precision

Directions: Choose at least two activities from the menu below. The activities must total 100 points. Place a checkmark next to each box to show which activities you will complete. All activities must be completed by _____ .

---

20 Points

❏ Create a Venn diagram to compare accuracy and precision.

❏ Make a folded quiz book in which you test if others can identify data that are accurate and precise but not necessarily both.

---

50 Points

❏ Create a scrapbook of newspaper articles with examples of accuracy and precision.

❏ Prepare a PowerPoint to explain whether it is more important to be accurate or to be precise in science. Include examples to support your view.

❏ Build an interactive museum exhibit for a children's museum that has visitors experiencing precise and accurate activities.

❏ **Free choice on accuracy and precision**—Prepare a proposal form and submit it to your teacher for approval.

---

80 Points

❏ Record a news report about a reporter who is incredibly precise, but not very accurate.

❏ Invent a new sport or activity that values precision rather than accuracy. Write a newspaper article or record a video about the sport, how it is played, and why precision is more important than accuracy when playing.

Dimensional Analysis

20-50-80 Menu

Objectives Covered Through This Menu and These Activities

- Students will use dimensional analysis to answer real-world questions.
- Students will be able to use dimensional analysis to convert between different units.
- Students will express and manipulate chemical quantities using chemical conventions and mathematical procedures.
- Students will communicate valid conclusions supported by data.

Materials Needed by Students for Completion

- Method for recording responses to word problems

Special Notes on the Use of This Menu

- This menu is a problem menu; it asks students to demonstrate their knowledge and answer one or more higher level word problems. It is set up in such a way that students will have to complete at least one of the higher level word problems. When introducing this menu, teachers will need to have already determined how they would like these problems completed and recorded for grading. Remember, this is the opportunity to hold high standards when it comes to showing work and defending answers!

Time Frame

- 1–2 weeks—Students are given a menu as the unit is started, and the teacher discusses all of the options on the menu. As the different options are discussed, students will choose the problems they are most interested in completing so that they meet their goal of 100 points. As the lessons progress through the week(s), the teacher and students refer back to the menu options associated with the content being taught.
- 1–2 days—The teacher chooses a problem from the menu to use with the entire class.

Suggested Forms

- All-purpose rubric
- Proposal form for point-based projects

Answers to Menu Problems

Problem 1: A Lamborghini can accelerate from 0 mph to 60 mph in 2.9 sec. If physical restrictions were not a limitation, how fast could the car be going in one minute at this rate of acceleration?

$$\frac{60 \text{ mph}}{2.9 \text{ sec}} \cdot \frac{60 \text{ sec}}{1 \text{ min}} = 1{,}241 \text{ mph in one minute}$$

$$\text{or } 1.2 \times 10^3 \text{ mph in one minute}$$

Problem 2: A student has decided to test the accuracy of her running trail. She has been told it is one mile in length. Because of limited supplies, and wanting an extra challenge, she has only a broken meter stick that is 43.8 cm in length to make the measurements. How many total ruler measurements will it be, including how many centimeters on the final measure, to check if her trail is one mile long?

$$\frac{5{,}280 \text{ ft}}{1 \text{ mi}} \cdot \frac{30.48 \text{ cm}}{1 \text{ ft}} \cdot \frac{1 \text{ ruler}}{43.8 \text{ cm}} = 3{,}674.3 \text{ rulers}$$

.3 of the 43.8 cm ruler remains as the final measurement. After multiplying these two measurements, she will need 13.1 cm more on the final measurement.

Problem 3: *The Queen Mary*, a registered cruise ship, has a volume of 151,200 gross registered tons (grt). The average volume of the adult human body is about $6.64 \times 10^{-2} \text{ m}^3$. If physical space and comfort were not a limitation, how many people could fit in *The Queen Mary*? If the average human weighs 152 lbs, how many kilograms would this be in total?

$$151{,}200 \text{ grt} \cdot \frac{2.83 \text{ m}^3}{1 \text{ grt}} \cdot \frac{1 \text{ human body}}{6.64 \times 10^{-2} \text{m}^3} = 6{,}444{,}217 \text{ humans}$$

$$6{,}444{,}217 \text{ humans} \cdot \frac{152 \text{ lbs}}{\text{human}} \cdot \frac{1 \text{ kg}}{2.20 \text{ lbs}} = 445{,}236{,}811 \text{ kg}$$

$$\text{or } 4.45 \times 10^8 \text{ kg}$$

Problem 4: The average corn crop in the Midwest yields 14 billion bushels per year. A bushel of corn is around 40–60 ears. Using this information, approximately how many ears of corn were harvested last year? If each corn cob has approximately 800 kernels in 16 rows, how many kernels of corn are in the average corn crop?

Calculate how many kernels were harvested:

$$\frac{14 \times 10^9 \text{ bushels}}{1 \text{ year}} \cdot \frac{40 \text{ ears}}{1 \text{ bushel}} = 5.6 \times 10^{11} \text{ ears}$$

$$\frac{14 \times 10^9 \text{ bushels}}{1 \text{ year}} \cdot \frac{60 \text{ ears}}{1 \text{ bushel}} = 8.4 \times 10^{11} \text{ ears}$$

Between 5.6×10^{11} and 8.4×10^{11} ears were harvested.

Calculate how many kernels of corn are in the average corn crop:

$$5.6 \times 10^{11} \text{ ears} \cdot \frac{800 \text{ kernels}}{1 \text{ ear}} = 4.48 \times 10^{14} \text{ kernels}$$

$$8.4 \times 10^{11} \text{ ears} \cdot \frac{800 \text{ kernels}}{1 \text{ ear}} = 6.72 \times 10^{14} \text{ kernels}$$

Between 4.48×10^{14} kernels and 6.72×10^{14} kernels are in the average corn crop.

Problem 5: Usain Bolt ran the 100 m sprint in 9.58 sec and the 200 m sprint in 19.19 sec. Based on these averages, is he faster or slower than an average elephant that can run at 24.15 mph?

$$\frac{100 \text{ m}}{9.58 \text{ sec}} \cdot \frac{60 \text{ sec}}{1 \text{ min}} \cdot \frac{60 \text{ min}}{1 \text{ hr}} \cdot \frac{1 \text{ mi}}{1609 \text{ m}} = \frac{23.36 \text{ mi}}{1 \text{ hr}}$$

$$\frac{200 \text{ m}}{19.19 \text{ sec}} \cdot \frac{60 \text{ sec}}{1 \text{ min}} \cdot \frac{60 \text{ min}}{1 \text{ hr}} \cdot \frac{1 \text{ mi}}{1609 \text{ m}} = \frac{23.32 \text{ mi}}{1 \text{ hr}}$$

Because an average elephant can run at 24.15 mph, and Usain Bolt's highest speed is 23.36 mph, he is slower than an elephant (for now).

Problem 6: A human heart beats an average of 1.17 beats per second. Each beat pumps between 60 mL and 90 mL of blood out of the heart. Based on this information, what is the range of liters of blood the heart pumps daily?

$$\frac{60 \text{ mL}}{1 \text{ beat}} \cdot \frac{1.17 \text{ beats}}{1 \text{ sec}} \cdot \frac{1 \text{ L}}{1,000 \text{ mL}} \cdot \frac{60 \text{ sec}}{1 \text{ min}} \cdot \frac{60 \text{ min}}{1 \text{ hr}} \cdot \frac{24 \text{ hrs}}{1 \text{ day}}$$

$$= 6,065 \text{ L per day or } 6.07 \times 10^3 \text{ L per day}$$

$$\frac{90 \text{ mL}}{1 \text{ beat}} \cdot \frac{1.17 \text{ beats}}{1 \text{ sec}} \cdot \frac{1 \text{ L}}{1,000 \text{ mL}} \cdot \frac{60 \text{ sec}}{1 \text{ min}} \cdot \frac{60 \text{ min}}{1 \text{ hr}} \cdot \frac{24 \text{ hrs}}{1 \text{ day}}$$

$$= 9,098 \text{ L per day or } 9.1 \times 10^3 \text{ L per day}$$

The heart pumps between 6,065 L and 9,098 L of blood each day.

Problem 7: A popular chocolate peanut candy bar maker uses exactly 16 peanuts in each of its candy bars. If this company can make 62 candy bars every 5 minutes at one factory that runs every day (except its founder's birthday) for 24 hours, how many pounds of peanuts does it use in that year? (*Note*: One pound of peanuts is approximately 82 peanuts.)

$$\frac{62 \text{ bars}}{5 \text{ min}} \cdot \frac{60 \text{ min}}{1 \text{ hr}} \cdot \frac{24 \text{ hrs}}{1 \text{ day}} \cdot 364 \text{ days} \left(365 - 1 \text{ for founder's birthday}\right) \cdot$$

$$\frac{16 \text{ peanuts}}{1 \text{ bar}} \cdot \frac{1 \text{ lb}}{82 \text{ peanuts}} = 1.27 \times 10^6 \text{ lbs of peanuts or}$$

$$1,268,212 \text{ lbs of peanuts}$$

Dimensional Analysis

Directions: Choose at least two activities from the menu below. The activities must total 100 points. Place a checkmark next to each box to show which activities you will complete. All activities must be completed by _____ .

---

20 Points

❑ **Problem 1:** A Lamborghini can accelerate from 0 mph to 60 mph in 2.9 sec. If physical restrictions were not a limitation, how fast could the car be going in one minute at this rate of acceleration?

❑ **Problem 2:** A student has decided to test the accuracy of her running trail. She has been told it is one mile in length. Because of limited supplies, and wanting an extra challenge, she has only a broken meter stick that is 43.8 cm in length to make the measurements. How many total ruler measurements will it be, including how many centimeters on the final measure, to check if her trail is one mile long?

---

50 Points

❑ **Problem 3:** *The Queen Mary*, a registered cruise ship, has a volume of 151,200 gross registered tons (grt). The average volume of the adult human body is about 6.64×10^{-2} m^3. If physical space and comfort were not a limitation, how many people could fit in *The Queen Mary*? If the average human weighs 152 lbs, how many kilograms would this be in total?

❑ **Problem 4:** The average corn crop in the Midwest yields 14 billion bushels per year. A bushel of corn is around 40–60 ears. Using this information, approximately how many ears of corn were harvested last year? If each corn cob has approximately 800 kernels in 16 rows, how many kernels of corn are in the average corn crop?

❑ **Problem 5:** Usain Bolt ran the 100 m sprint in 9.58 sec and the 200 m sprint in 19.19 sec. Based on these averages, is he faster or slower than an average elephant that can run at 24.15 mph?

❑ **Free choice on practicing dimensional analysis calculations**—Prepare a proposal form and submit it to your teacher for approval.

Dimensional Analysis, continued

80 Points

❒ **Problem 6:** A human heart beats an average of 1.17 beats per second. Each beat pumps between 60 mL and 90 mL of blood out of the heart. Based on this information, what is the range of liters of blood the heart pumps daily?

❒ **Problem 7:** A popular chocolate peanut candy bar maker uses exactly 16 peanuts in each of its candy bars. If this company can make 62 candy bars every 5 minutes at one factory that runs every day (except its founder's birthday) for 24 hours, how many pounds of peanuts does it use in that year? (*Note*: One pound of peanuts is approximately 82 peanuts.)

CHAPTER 6

Atomic Theory

 DOI: 10.4324/9781003234357-8

20 Points
▢ _____
▢ _____
50 Points
▢ _____
▢ _____
▢ _____
▢ _____
80 Points
▢ _____
▢ _____

Atomic Theory

20-50-80 Menu

Objectives Covered Through This Menu and These Activities

- Students will be able to describe the experimental design and conclusions used in the development of modern atomic theory, including Dalton's Postulates, Thomson's discovery of electron properties, Rutherford's nuclear atom, and Bohr's nuclear atom.
- Students will communicate valid conclusions supported by data.
- Students will describe the history of chemistry and contributions of scientists.

Materials Needed by Students for Completion

- Poster board or large white paper
- Materials for three-dimensional timelines
- Blank index cards (for trading cards)
- Materials for board games (folders, colored cards, etc.)
- Recording software or application (for documentary)

Special Notes on the Use of This Menu

- This menu gives students the opportunity to create a documentary. The grading and sharing of these products can often be facilitated by having students prerecord their product using whatever technology is most convenient for the teacher. This allows the teacher to decide when it will be shown as well as keeps the presentation to its intended length. If recording options are limited, this activity can be modified by allowing students to act out the product (like a play) in front of the class.

Time Frame

- 1–2 weeks—Students are given a menu as the unit is started, and the teacher discusses all of the product options on the menu. As the different options are discussed, students will choose the activities they are most interested in completing so that they meet their goal of 100 points. As the lessons progress through the week(s), the teacher and students refer back to the menu options associated with the content being taught.

- 1–2 days—The teacher chooses an activity or product from the menu to use with the entire class.

Suggested Forms

- All-purpose rubric
- Proposal form for point-based projects

Atomic Theory

Directions: Choose at least two activities from the menu below. The activities must total 100 points. Place a checkmark next to each box to show which activities you will complete. All activities must be completed by _____ .

---

20 Points

❒ Build a three-dimensional timeline that shows how atomic theory has changed through time.

❒ Write a children's book that tells the story of how our knowledge about the structure of the atom has changed over time.

---

50 Points

❒ You are Ernest Rutherford. Prepare a You Be the Person presentation in which you come to class as Rutherford and discuss your work in atomic theory. Be prepared to discuss what scientists knew before your work, what you have discovered (and how), and its implications for the future.

❒ Pretend that scientists could be as famous as athletes, and create a set of trading cards for the different scientists who contributed to atomic theory. In addition to their "stats," include at least one quote about their work on each card.

❒ Invent a board game that allows your classmates to take on the roles of the different atomic theorists as they progress through their discoveries.

❒ **Free choice on atomic theory**—Prepare a proposal form and submit it to your teacher for approval.

---

80 Points

❒ Write a choose-your-own-adventure story in which readers begin in Greece and make choices as they become different scientists who contributed to the atomic theory. Your story should have a real-world ending as well as other endings that do not lead to our current knowledge of atomic theory.

❒ Record a documentary about the people "behind the scenes." Scientists rarely work in isolation. Research the people who supported the scientists credited with atomic theory discoveries and tell their story, including their contributions.

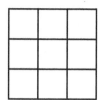

Isotopes

Tic-Tac-Toe Menu

Objectives Covered Through This Menu and These Activities

- Students will be able to recognize how an isotope differs from an atom noted on the periodic table.
- Students will be able to calculate average atomic mass of an element using isotopic composition.
- Students will express and manipulate chemical quantities using chemical conventions and mathematical procedures.
- Students will communicate valid conclusions supported by data.

Materials Needed by Students for Completion

- Poster board or large white paper
- Microsoft PowerPoint or other slideshow software
- Recording software or application (for informational video)
- Internet access (for WebQuests)
- Large blank lined index cards (for instruction cards)
- Method for recording responses to word problems

Special Notes on the Use of This Menu

- This menu is a product and problem menu; it asks students to not only create products to demonstrate their knowledge but also answer one or more higher level word problems. It is set up in such a way that students will have to complete at least one of the word problems. When introducing this menu, teachers will need to have already determined how they would like these problems completed and recorded for grading. Remember, this is the opportunity to hold high standards when it comes to showing work and defending answers!
- This menu gives students the opportunity to create an instructional video. The grading and sharing of these products can often be facilitated by having students prerecord their product using whatever technology is most convenient for the teacher. This allows the teacher to decide when it will be shown as well as keeps the presentation to its intended length. If recording options are limited, this activity can be modified by allowing students to act out the product (like a play) in front of the class.

- This menu allows students to create a WebQuest. There are multiple versions and templates for WebQuests available on the Internet. It is your decision whether you would like to specify a format or if you will allow students to create one of their own choosing.
- This menu gives students the opportunity to teach a concept. This can take a significant amount of time and organization. It can save time if the students who choose to do a lesson can sign up for a designated day and time that is determined when the menu is distributed.

Time Frame

- 2–3 weeks—Students are given the menu as the unit is started. The teacher will go over all of the options for that content and have students place checkmarks in the boxes that represent the activities they are most interested in completing. As students choose activities, they should complete a column or a row. When students complete this pattern, they have completed one activity from each content area, learning style, or level of Bloom's revised taxonomy, depending on the design of the menu. As the teacher presents lessons throughout the week, he or she should refer back to the menu options associated with that content.
- 1 week—At the start of the unit, the teacher chooses the three activities he or she feels are most valuable for students. Stations can be set up in the classroom. These three activities are available for student choice throughout the week as regular instruction takes place.
- 1–2 days—The teacher chooses an activity from the menu to use with the entire class.

Suggested Forms

- All-purpose rubric
- Student-taught lesson rubric
- Free-choice proposal form

Answers to Menu Problems

Problem 1: Two isotopes of rubidium occur naturally—rubidium-85 (mass of 84.91 amu) and rubidium-87 (mass of 86.91 amu). Rubidium-85 has an abundance of 72.15%. Calculate the average atomic mass of the two isotopes.

$$\text{Rubidium-85: } 84.91 \text{ amu} \cdot \frac{72.15}{100} = 61.26 \text{ amu}$$

$$\text{Rubidium-87: } 86.91 \text{ amu} \cdot \frac{100 - 72.15}{100} = 24.20 \text{ amu}$$

$$\text{Average atomic mass} = 61.26 \text{ amu} + 24.20 \text{ amu} = 85.46 \text{ amu}$$

Problem 2: Copper has two naturally occurring isotopes—copper-63 (mass of 62.93 amu) and copper-65. Copper-63 has an abundance of 69.17%. Using the periodic table, find the mass of the copper-65.

$$\text{Copper-63: } 62.93 \text{ amu} \cdot \frac{69.17}{100} = 43.53 \text{ amu}$$

Copper-65 has an abundance of $100 - 69.17 = 30.83\%$.

$$\text{Atomic mass from periodic table} = \left(\text{abundance of } {}^{63}\text{Cu}\right)\left(\text{mass of } {}^{63}\text{Cu}\right) + \left(\text{abundance of } {}^{65}\text{Cu}\right)\left(\text{mass of } {}^{65}\text{Cu}\right)$$

$$63.55 \text{ amu} = 43.53 \text{ amu} + \left(\frac{30.83}{100}\right)(\text{mass})$$

$$-43.53 \text{ amu} \qquad -43.53 \text{ amu}$$

$$\frac{20.02 \text{ amu}}{.3083} = \frac{(.3083)(\text{mass})}{.3083}$$

$$64.94 \text{ amu} = \text{mass}$$

The mass of copper-65 is 64.94 amu.

Problem 3: Gallium has two isotopes—gallium-69 (mass of 68.93 amu) and gallium-71 (mass of 70.92 amu). Using the average mass on the periodic table, calculate the abundance of each isotope.

$$\text{Gallium-69: } \left(\frac{x}{100}\right)\left(68.93 \text{ amu}\right)$$

$$\text{Gallium-71: } \left(\frac{100 - x}{100}\right)\left(70.92 \text{ amu}\right)$$

Atomic mass from periodic table $= \left(\text{abundance of } ^{69}\text{Ga} \right) \left(\text{mass of } ^{69}\text{Ga} \right) +$

$$\left(\text{abundance of } ^{71}\text{Ga} \right) \left(\text{mass of } ^{71}\text{Ga} \right)$$

$$100 \left[69.72 \text{ amu} = \left(\frac{x}{100} \right) (68.83) + \left(\frac{100-x}{100} \right) (70.92) \right]$$

$$6972 = (68.93)(x) + (100-x)(70.92)$$

$$\begin{aligned} 6972 &= 68.93x + 7092 - 70.92x \\ -\,7092 &\quad\; -\,7092 \end{aligned}$$

$$\frac{-120}{-1.99} = \frac{-1.99x}{-1.99}$$

$$60.30 = x$$

Gallium-69 = 60.30%

Gallium-71 = 39.70%

Isotopes

Directions: Check the boxes you plan to complete. They should form a tic-tac-toe across or down. All products are due by: _____ .

☐ *What Is an Isotope?* Write an instruction card that explains how to determine if an atom is an isotope or not.	☐ *Problem 1* Two isotopes of rubidium occur naturally—rubidium-85 (mass of 84.91 amu) and rubidium-87 (mass of 86.91 amu). Rubidium-85 has an abundance of 72.15%. Calculate the average atomic mass of the two isotopes.	☐ *Teach Others About Isotopes* Prepare a student-taught lesson to teach others about the relationship between abundance of isotopes, atomic mass of isotopes, and average atomic mass.
☐ *Teach Others About Isotopes* Develop a PowerPoint or WebQuest that others could use to understand more about isotopes and their abundances.	☐ **Free Choice: What Is an Isotope?** (Fill out your proposal form before beginning the free choice!)	☐ *Problem 2* Copper has two naturally occurring isotopes—copper-63 (mass of 62.93 amu) and copper-65. Copper-63 has an abundance of 69.17%. Using the periodic table, find the mass of the copper-65.
☐ *Problem 3* Gallium has two isotopes—gallium-69 (mass of 68.93 amu) and gallium-71 (mass of 70.92 amu). Using the average mass on the periodic table, calculate the abundance of each isotope.	☐ *Teach Others About Isotopes* Record an instructional video to teach others how information on the periodic table can be used to calculate information about commonly occurring isotopes.	☐ *What Is an Isotope?* Create a folded quiz book to test your classmates' ability to identify isotopes using a mass and the periodic table.

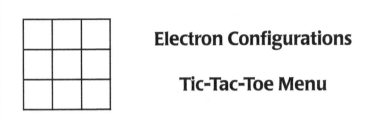

Electron Configurations

Tic-Tac-Toe Menu

Objectives Covered Through This Menu and These Activities

- Students will be able to express the arrangement of electrons in atoms of representative elements using electron configurations and Lewis valence electron dot structures.
- Students will express and manipulate chemical quantities using chemical conventions and mathematical procedures.

Materials Needed by Students for Completion

- Poster board or large white paper
- Large blank lined index cards (for instruction cards)
- Blank index cards (for trading cards and concentration cards)
- Recording software or application (for instructional videos)
- Lewis Dot Cube template

Special Notes on the Use of This Menu

- This menu gives students the opportunity to create an instructional video. The grading and sharing of these products can often be facilitated by having students prerecord their product using whatever technology is most convenient for the teacher. This allows the teacher to decide when it will be shown as well as keeps the presentation to its intended length. If recording options are limited, this activity can be modified by allowing students to act out the product (like a play) in front of the class.

Time Frame

- 2–3 weeks—Students are given the menu as the unit is started. The teacher will go over all of the options for that content and have students place checkmarks in the boxes that represent the activities they are most interested in completing. As students choose activities, they should complete a column or a row. When students complete this pattern, they have completed one activity from each content area, learning style, or level of Bloom's revised taxonomy, depending on the design of the menu. As the teacher presents lessons throughout the week, he or she should refer back to the menu options associated with that content.

- 1 week—At the start of the unit, the teacher chooses the three activities he or she feels are most valuable for students. Stations can be set up in the classroom. These three activities are available for student choice throughout the week as regular instruction takes place.
- 1–2 days—The teacher chooses an activity from the menu to use with the entire class.

Suggested Forms

- All-purpose rubric
- Free-choice proposal form

Name:_____ Date:_____

Electron Configurations

Directions: Check the boxes you plan to complete. They should form a tic-tac-toe across or down. All products are due by: _____ .

☐ *Valence Electrons* Prepare a valence electron brochure. Your brochure should include where they are located, their role in chemical reactions, and how we can calculate how many an atom or ion will have.	☐ *Lewis Dot* Design and fold a cube that shows the Lewis dot configurations for a cation, an anion, a polyatomic ion, a noble gas, a halogen, and a transition metal.	☐ *Electron Configurations* Assemble a set of concentration cards that has players matching electron configurations with their element or ions.
☐ *Electron Configurations* Record an instructional video in which you teach others how to write electron configurations. Be sure to use examples that include ions, as well as the "d" and "f" blocks.	☐ **Free Choice:** **Valence Electrons** (Fill out your proposal form before beginning the free choice!)	☐ *Lewis Dot* Make a folded quiz book in which players must examine Lewis dot structures and identify the substance being shown.
☐ *Lewis Dot* Write an instruction card that explains how to create a Lewis dot diagram for different types of substances, including different types of ions and elements.	☐ *Electron Configurations* Create a set of electron configuration trading cards for at least 10 different elements with different configurations. The cards should include configurations for each atom's neutral state as well as any ions.	☐ *Valence Electrons* Record and perform an original song about valence electrons. Your song should explain where they are located, their role in chemistry, and how we can calculate how many an atom or ion will have.

© Taylor & Francis • *Differentiating I   nstruction With Menus: Chemistry* • *Grades 9–12*

Lewis Dot Cube

Design and fold a cube that shows the Lewis dot configurations for a cation, an anion, a polyatomic ion, a noble gas, a halogen, and a transition metal.

Electromagnetic Spectrum

Meal Menu

Objectives Covered Through This Menu and These Activities

- Students will be able to describe the different waves found on the electromagnet spectrum.
- Students will be able to describe the mathematical relationships between energy, frequency, and wavelength of light using the electromagnetic spectrum.
- Students will express and manipulate chemical quantities using chemical conventions and mathematical procedures.
- Students will communicate valid conclusions supported by data.
- Students will describe the history of chemistry and contributions of scientists.

Materials Needed by Students for Completion

- Poster board or large white paper
- Blank index cards (for trading cards)
- Recording software or application (for videos)
- Internet access (for WebQuests)
- Electromagnetic Wave Cube template
- Large blank lined index cards (for instruction cards)
- Method for recording responses to word problems

Special Notes on the Use of This Menu

- This menu is a product and problem menu; it asks students to not only create products to demonstrate their knowledge but also answer one or more higher level word problems. It is set up in such a way that students will have to complete at least one of the word problems. When introducing this menu, teachers will need to have already determined how they would like these problems completed and recorded for grading. Remember, this is the opportunity to hold high standards when it comes to showing work and defending answers!
- This menu gives students the opportunity to create a video. The grading and sharing of these products can often be facilitated by having students prerecord their product using whatever technology is most convenient for the teacher. This allows the teacher to decide when it

will be shown as well as keeps the presentation to its intended length. If recording options are limited, this activity can be modified by allowing students to act out the product (like a play) in front of the class.
- This menu gives students the opportunity to facilitate a class model. The expectation is that all students in the classroom will play an active role in the model. This may mean that students need some additional space for their model.
- This menu allows students to create a WebQuest. There are multiple versions and templates for WebQuests available on the Internet. It is your decision whether you would like to specify a format or if you will allow students to create one of their own choosing.

Time Frame
- 2–3 weeks—Students are given the menu as the unit is started. As the lesson or unit progresses throughout the week, students should refer back to the menu options associated with that content. The teacher will go over all of the options for that objective and have students place a checkmark in the box for each option that represents the activity they are most interested in completing. As teaching continues, the activities chosen and completed should create a full day's meal, with a breakfast, a lunch, a dinner, and an optional dessert. The teacher may choose to allow students time to work after other work is finished. When students complete the menu with this expectation, they have completed one activity from each content area, learning style, or level of Bloom's revised taxonomy, depending on the design of the menu.
- 1 week—At the start of the unit, the teacher chooses one activity from each meal family he or she feels is most valuable for students. Stations can be set up in the classroom. These three activities are available for student choice throughout the week as regular instruction takes place.
- 1–2 days—The teacher chooses an activity or product from an objective to use with the entire class during that lesson time. Additionally, the teacher could choose one of the two desserts as an enrichment activity.

Suggested Forms
- All-purpose rubric
- Free-choice proposal form

Answers to Menu Problems

Problem 1: How many minutes would it take a radio wave to travel from the planet Mars to Earth?

Given that Mars is approximately 54.6 million km from Earth:

$$5.46 \times 10^8 \text{ km} \cdot \frac{1,000 \text{ m}}{1 \text{ km}} = 5.46 \times 10^{11} \text{ m}$$

$$5.46 \times 10^{11} \text{ m} \cdot \frac{1 \text{ sec}}{2.998 \times 10^8 \text{ m}} \cdot \frac{1 \text{ min}}{60 \text{ sec}} = 30.4 \text{ sec}$$

It would take 30.4 sec.

Problem 2: If a scuba diver is 28 m below the surface, how long would it take for a sound wave to reach him from the surface, assuming the temperature of the water is between 20° C and 25° C?

$$28 \text{ m} \cdot \frac{1 \text{ sec}}{1.498 \times 10^3 \text{ m}} = .019 \text{ sec}$$

It would take .019 sec or 1.9×10^{-2} sec.

Problem 3: Two students are debating about the color of light being emitted from a screen. The light has an energy of 4.41×10^{-18} J. What is the color of the light?

$$\varepsilon = hv$$

$$\frac{4.41 \times 10^{-18} \text{ J}}{6.626 \times 10^{-34} \text{ J}} = \frac{\left(6.626 \times 10^{-34} \text{ J}\right)v}{6.626 \times 10^{-34} \text{ J}}$$

$$6.66 \times 10^{15} \text{ Hz} = v$$

The light is blue.

Electromagnetic Spectrum

Directions: Choose one activity each for breakfast, lunch, and dinner. Dessert is an activity you can choose to do after you have finished your other meals. All products must be completed by: _____ .

Breakfast

- ❑ Create a set of trading cards for the waves of the electromagnetic spectrum.
- ❑ Make an instruction card that explains how to determine an electromagnetic wave based on its properties.
- ❑ Assemble a product cube with information about each type of electromagnetic wave on each side.

Lunch

- ❑ **Problem 1:** How many minutes would it take a radio wave to travel from the planet Mars to Earth?
- ❑ **Problem 2:** If a scuba diver is 28 m below the surface, how long would it take for a sound wave to reach him from the surface, assuming the temperature of the water is between 20 °C and 25 °C?
- ❑ **Problem 3:** Two students are debating about the color of light being emitted from a screen. The light has an energy of 4.41×10^{-18} J. What is the color of the light?

Dinner

- ❑ A red photon has decided it no longer wants to be red; it dreams of running with the ultraviolet photons. Write a letter to the red photon explaining what would have to change in order to achieve its dream. Be sure to include practical advice about how it could be possible as well as calculations!
- ❑ Prepare a WebQuest that allows questors to investigate different aspects of the electromagnetic spectrum as well as perform calculations using the waves' properties.
- ❑ Invent a classroom model that could be used to demonstrate the properties of all of the waves on the electromagnetic spectrum.

Dessert

- ❑ Free choice on the electromagnet spectrum—Prepare a proposal form and submit it to your teacher for approval.
- ❑ Record a video to teach your classmates about interesting, yet not commonly known information about the electromagnetic spectrum.

Electromagnetic Wave Cube

Assemble a product cube with information about each type of electromagnetic wave on each side.

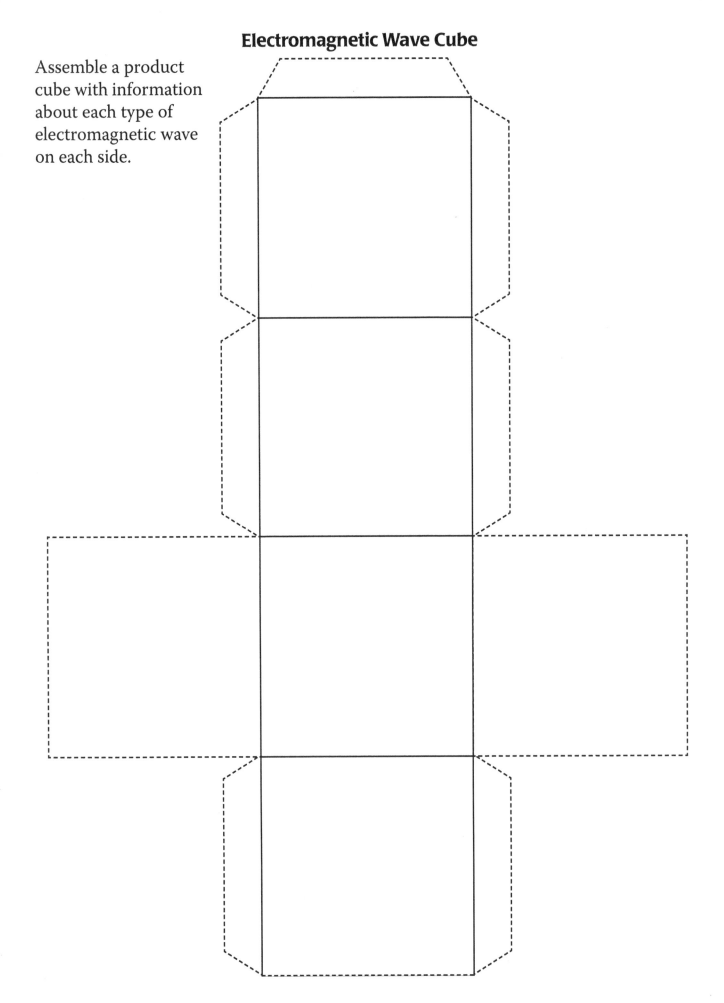

CHAPTER 7

Matter

DOI: 10.4324/9781003234357-9

20 Points
□ _____
□ _____
50 Points
□ _____
□ _____
□ _____
□ _____
80 Points
□ _____
□ _____

Classifying Matter

20-50-80 Menu

Objectives Covered Through This Menu and These Activities

- Students will be able to classify matter as pure substances or mixtures through investigation of their properties.
- Students will plan and implement procedures.
- Students will collect data and make measurements with accuracy and precision.
- Students will express and manipulate chemical quantities using chemical conventions and mathematical procedures.
- Students will communicate valid conclusions supported by data.

Materials Needed by Students for Completion

- Poster board or large white paper
- Recording software or application (for videos)
- Magazines (for collages)
- Recycled materials (for museum exhibits and models)

Special Notes on the Use of This Menu

- This menu gives students the opportunity to create a video. The grading and sharing of these products can often be facilitated by having students prerecord their product using whatever technology is most convenient for the teacher. This allows the teacher to decide when it will be shown as well as keeps the presentation to its intended length. If recording options are limited, this activity can be modified by allowing students to act out the product (like a play) in front of the class.
- This menu asks students to use recycled materials to create their museum exhibit and model. This does not mean only plastic and paper; instead, students should focus on using materials in new ways. It works well if a box is started for "recycled" contributions at the beginning of the school year. That way, students always have access to these types of materials.

Time Frame

- 1–2 weeks—Students are given a menu as the unit is started, and the teacher discusses all of the product options on the menu. As the different options are discussed, students will choose the activities they are most interested in completing so that they meet their goal of 100 points. As the lessons progress through the week(s), the teacher and students refer back to the menu options associated with the content being taught.

- 1–2 days—The teacher chooses an activity or product from the menu to use with the entire class.

Suggested Forms

- All-purpose rubric
- Proposal form for point-based projects

Name:_____ Date:_____

Classifying Matter

Directions: Choose at least two activities from the menu below. The activities must total 100 points. Place a checkmark next to each box to show which activities you will complete. All activities must be completed by _____ .

---

20 Points

❏ Make a window pane to show the different ways we can classify matter.

❏ Assemble a collage with examples of the different classifications of matter.

---

50 Points

❏ Create a model that could be used to illustrate the differences between pure substances and the different types of mixtures.

❏ Design a social media page for a mixture that only likes to interact with other substances that have similar properties.

❏ Assemble a children's museum exhibit that could teach children about how to classify matter.

❏ **Free choice on classifying matter**—Prepare a proposal form and submit it to your teacher for approval.

---

80 Points

❏ Write five journal entries for a pure substance that is being forced to become part of a heterogenous mixture.

❏ Record a video of an original investigation of different substances and their properties. Your investigation should teach others about the properties you are investigating.

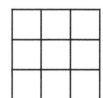

Properties and Changes

Tic-Tac-Toe Menu

Objectives Covered Through This Menu and These Activities

- Students will be able to identify extensive properties, such as mass and volume, and intensive properties, such as density and melting points.
- Students will be able to differentiate between physical and chemical changes and properties.
- Students will communicate valid conclusions supported by data.
- Students will critique scientific explanations and evaluate the impact of research on scientific thought.

Materials Needed by Students for Completion

- Poster board or large white paper
- Materials for board games (folders, colored cards, etc.)
- Blank index cards (for card sorts)
- Internet access (for WebQuests)
- Properties Cube template
- Scrapbooking materials
- Materials for bulletin board display
- Large blank lined index cards (for instruction cards)

Special Notes on the Use of This Menu

- This menu allows students to create a bulletin board display. Some classrooms may only have one bulletin board, so the teacher can divide the board into sections, or additional classroom wall or hall space can be sectioned off for the creation of these displays. Students can plan their display based on the amount of space they are assigned.
- This menu allows students to create a WebQuest. There are multiple versions and templates for WebQuests available on the Internet. It is your decision whether you would like to specify a format or if you will allow students to create one of their own choosing.

Time Frame

- 2–3 weeks—Students are given the menu as the unit is started. The teacher will go over all of the options for that content and have students place checkmarks in the boxes that represent the activities they are most interested in completing. As students choose activities, they should complete a column or a row. When students complete this pattern, they have completed one activity from each content area, learning style, or level of Bloom's revised taxonomy, depending on the design of the menu. As the teacher presents lessons throughout the week, he or she should refer back to the menu options associated with that content.

- 1 week—At the start of the unit, the teacher chooses the three activities he or she feels are most valuable for students. Stations can be set up in the classroom. These three activities are available for student choice throughout the week as regular instruction takes place.
- 1–2 days—The teacher chooses an activity from the menu to use with the entire class.

Suggested Forms

- All-purpose rubric
- Free-choice proposal form

Name:_____ Date:_____

Properties and Changes

Directions: Check the boxes you plan to complete. They should form a tic-tac-toe across or down. All products are due by: _____ .

☐ *Physical and Chemical Changes* Create a card sort to practice recognizing physical and chemical changes that we observe daily.	☐ *Extensive and Intensive Properties* Make a social media profile for an element of your choice. Include information about its extensive and intensive properties as part of its "About Me" section.	☐ *Physical and Chemical Properties* Design a bulletin board display that could teach your classmates about the chemistry behind physical and chemical properties.
☐ *Physical and Chemical Properties* Assemble two product cubes, one with examples of physical properties, and one with examples of chemical properties.	☐ **Free Choice: Physical and Chemical Changes** (Fill out your proposal form before beginning the free choice!)	☐ *Extensive and Intensive Properties* Choose a substance and prepare a song or rap about its extensive and intensive properties as well as how you determined each.
☐ *Extensive and Intensive Properties* Design a WebQuest in which users visit different websites to watch videos and make observations about the extensive and intensive properties of everyday objects.	☐ *Physical and Chemical Properties* Assemble a scrapbook of objects with unusual or commonly confused physical and chemical properties.	☐ *Physical and Chemical Changes* Write an acrostic for the words *physical* and *chemical*. Record examples of physical changes for the word *physical* and chemical changes for the word *chemical*.

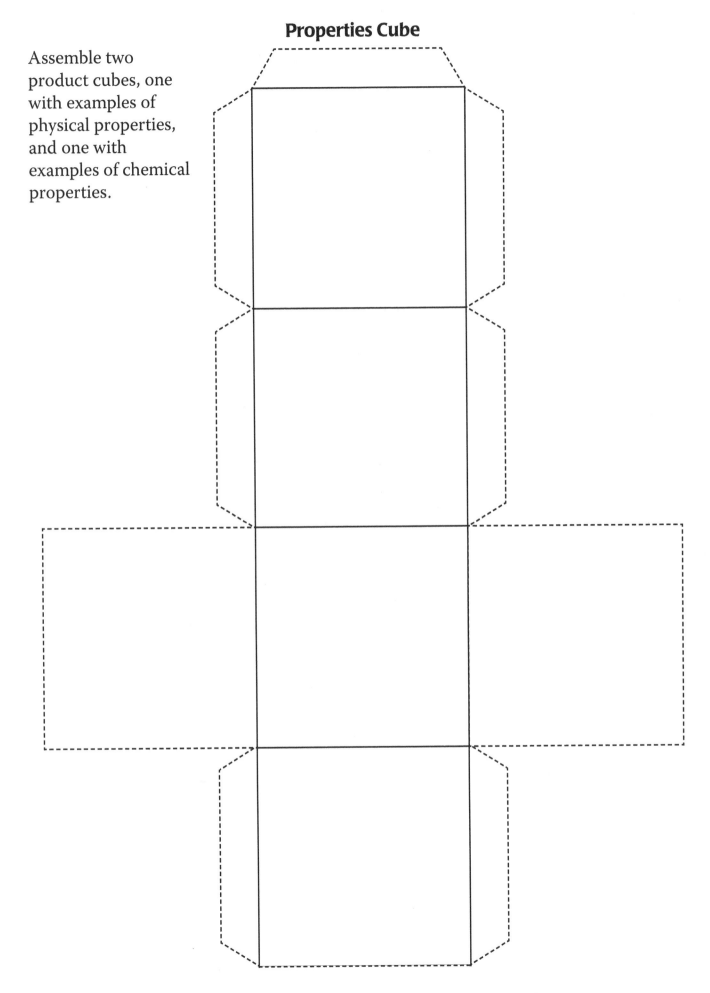

Properties Cube

Assemble two product cubes, one with examples of physical properties, and one with examples of chemical properties.

© Taylor & Francis • *Differentiating I   nstruction With Menus: Chemistry • Grades 9–12*

....

Families of the Periodic Table

20-50-80 Menu

Objectives Covered Through This Menu and These Activities

- Students will be able to identify and explain the properties of chemical families, including alkali metals, alkaline earth metals, halogens, noble gases, and transition metals, using the periodic table.
- Students will critique scientific explanations and evaluate the impact of research on scientific thought.
- Students will describe the history of chemistry and contributions of scientists.

Materials Needed by Students for Completion

- Poster board or large white paper
- Blank index cards (for mobiles, trading cards)
- Recording software or application (for videos)
- Scrapbooking materials
- Recycled materials (for museum exhibits)

Special Notes on the Use of This Menu

- This menu gives students the opportunity to create a video. The grading and sharing of these products can often be facilitated by having students prerecord their product using whatever technology is most convenient for the teacher. This allows the teacher to decide when it will be shown as well as keeps the presentation to its intended length. If recording options are limited, this activity can be modified by allowing students to act out the product (like a play) in front of the class.
- This menu asks students to use recycled materials to create their museum exhibits. This does not mean only plastic and paper; instead, students should focus on using materials in new ways. It works well if a box is started for "recycled" contributions at the beginning of the school year. That way, students always have access to these types of materials.

Time Frame

- 1–2 weeks—Students are given a menu as the unit is started, and the teacher discusses all of the product options on the menu. As the different options are discussed, students will choose the activities they are most interested in completing so that they meet their goal of 100 points. As the lessons progress through the week(s), the teacher and students refer back to the menu options associated with the content being taught.

- 1–2 days—The teacher chooses an activity or product from the menu to use with the entire class.

Suggested Forms

- All-purpose rubric
- Proposal form for point-based projects

Name:_____ Date:_____

Families of the Periodic Table

Directions: Choose at least two activities from the menu below. The activities must total 100 points. Place a checkmark next to each box to show which activities you will complete. All activities must be completed by _____ .

---

20 Points

❑ Create a set of trading cards for the families in the periodic table. Be sure to include information about their chemical properties as well as what makes each family unique.

❑ Design a periodic table museum exhibit that shares information about each of the families on the periodic table.

---

50 Points

❑ Create a triple Venn diagram to compare three of the families of the periodic table.

❑ Record a video in which you make the chemical properties of the periodic table families fun to learn and easy to remember.

❑ The periodic table is feeling nostalgic. Assemble a family scrapbook that features all of its family members and their unique qualities.

❑ **Free choice on families of the periodic table**—Prepare a proposal form and submit it to your teacher for approval.

---

80 Points

❑ Create a children's book in which there is a disagreement between two of the families of the periodic table, and they get their chemical properties involved to settle the dispute.

❑ Design a social media profile for one of the periodic table families. Your family needs to be friends and interact with the other families on its social media page.

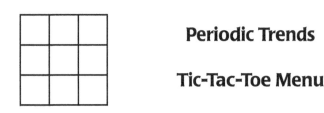

Periodic Trends

Tic-Tac-Toe Menu

Objectives Covered Through This Menu and These Activities

- Students will interpret periodic trends, including atomic radius, electronegativity, and ionization energy, using the Periodic Table.
- Students will be able to explain the use of chemical and physical properties in the historical development of the Periodic Table.
- Students will critique scientific explanations and evaluate the impact of research on scientific thought.
- Students will describe the history of chemistry and contributions of scientists.

Materials Needed by Students for Completion

- Poster board or large white paper
- Blank index cards (for card sorts)
- Materials for three-dimensional timelines
- Recording software or application (for informational videos)
- Ruler (for comic strips)

Special Notes on the Use of This Menu

- This menu gives students the opportunity to create an informational video. The grading and sharing of these products can often be facilitated by having students prerecord their product using whatever technology is most convenient for the teacher. This allows the teacher to decide when it will be shown as well as keeps the presentation to its intended length. If recording options are limited, this activity can be modified by allowing students to act out the product (like a play) in front of the class.

Time Frame

- 2–3 weeks—Students are given the menu as the unit is started. The teacher will go over all of the options for that content and have students place checkmarks in the boxes that represent the activities they are most interested in completing. As students choose activities, they should complete a column or a row. When students complete this pattern, they have completed one activity from each content area, learning style, or level of Bloom's revised taxonomy, depending on the design of the menu. As the teacher presents lessons throughout the week, he or she should refer back to the menu options associated with that content.

- 1 week—At the start of the unit, the teacher chooses the three activities he or she feels are most valuable for students. Stations can be set up in the classroom. These three activities are available for student choice throughout the week as regular instruction takes place.
- 1–2 days—The teacher chooses an activity from the menu to use with the entire class.

Suggested Forms

- All-purpose rubric
- Free-choice proposal form

Periodic Trends

Directions: Check the boxes you plan to complete. They should form a tic-tac-toe across or down. All products are due by: _____ .

☐ *Development of Periodic Table* Prepare a You Be the Person presentation in which you are Henry Moseley. Discuss your thoughts on the periodic table and your thoughts on its design.	☐ *Trends in the Periodic Table* Make a folded quiz book to quiz others on the periodic table trends. It should ask them to make predictions about atoms and ions based on periodic trends.	☐ *Atomic Radii* Prepare a poster that explains why and how atomic radii change in families and periods. Include at least two examples that illustrate the trend.
☐ *Electronegativity* Draw a creative comic strip that illustrates electronegativity and how it trends on the periodic table.	☐ **Free Choice: Development of Periodic Table** (Fill out your proposal form before beginning the free choice!)	☐ *Trends in the Periodic Table* Design a quiz (with an answer key) about predicting periodic trends for different atoms and ions. Include multiple levels of questions from more basic to challenging.
☐ *Trends in the Periodic Table* Create a card sort in which players must sort atoms and ions for each of the periodic trends we are studying. Be sure and include some tricky items!	☐ *Ionization Energy* Record an informational video about ionization energy as a trend in the periodic table. Include examples that support your commentary.	☐ *Development of Periodic Table* Assemble a three-dimensional timeline for the development of the periodic table. Be sure to include how different scientists used physical and chemical properties in its development.

Phase Diagrams

20-50-80 Menu

Objectives Covered Through This Menu and These Activities

- Students will be able to interpret phase diagrams, including identifying states of matter, melting and freezing points, and the triple and critical point.
- Students will communicate valid conclusions supported by data.

Materials Needed by Students for Completion

- Poster board or large white paper
- Microsoft PowerPoint or other slideshow software
- Internet access (for WebQuests)

Special Notes on the Use of This Menu

- This menu gives students the opportunity to facilitate a class game. The expectation is that all students in the classroom will play an active role in the game. This may mean that the facilitator may need some additional space and time for his or her game. This can take a significant amount of time and organization. It can save time if all of the students who choose to present their game can sign up for a designated day and time that is determined when the menu is distributed.
- This menu allows students to create a WebQuest. There are multiple versions and templates for WebQuests available on the Internet. It is your decision whether you would like to specify a format or if you will allow students to create one of their own choosing.

Time Frame

- 1–2 weeks—Students are given a menu as the unit is started, and the teacher discusses all of the product options on the menu. As the different options are discussed, students will choose the activities they are most interested in completing so that they meet their goal of 100 points. As the lessons progress through the week(s), the teacher and students refer back to the menu options associated with the content being taught.
- 1–2 days—The teacher chooses an activity or product from the menu to use with the entire class.

Suggested Forms
- All-purpose rubric
- Proposal form for point-based projects

Phase Diagrams

Directions: Choose at least two activities from the menu below. The activities must total 100 points. Place a checkmark next to each box to show which activities you will complete. All activities must be completed by _____ .

20 Points

- ☐ Prepare a poster that shows a phase diagram. Label each area of the diagram, each line, and the triple and critical points. Provide a definition for each label. Don't forget to label your axes!

- ☐ Design a PowerPoint presentation that demonstrates how to draw each part of a phase diagram.

50 Points

- ☐ Write your own worksheet about interpreting phase diagrams. This should be original work, not taken from a preexisting source.

- ☐ Create a WebQuest that focuses on the experiments conducted to gather data for and support the creation of phase diagrams.

- ☐ Propose an original class game that could help your classmates practice their phase diagram interpretation skills.

- ☐ **Free choice on interpreting phase diagrams**—Prepare a proposal form and submit it to your teacher for approval.

80 Points

- ☐ Consider the construction and conceptualization of a phase diagram. Based on your observations, invent an original *nonchemical* phase diagram using the concepts of relationships and changes. After labeling all of the data provided, prepare an explanation of your diagram.

- ☐ A carbon dioxide molecule at STP has decided it has had enough of its current state. It wants to seek new adventure—embracing change and new experiences. Write a story about this molecule's experiences as it approaches different states and "points" in its adventure. Although creative, your story must be chemically accurate.

Gas Laws

Game Show Menu

Objectives Covered Through This Menu and These Activities

- Students will be able to describe the relationships between volume, pressure, number of moles, and temperature.
- Students will be able to calculate changes using Boyle's law, Charles's law, Avogadro's law, Dalton's law of partial pressure, combined gas law, and the ideal gas law.
- Students will plan and implement procedures.
- Students will collect data and make measurements with accuracy and precision.
- Students will express and manipulate chemical quantities using chemical conventions and mathematical procedures.
- Students will communicate valid conclusions supported by data.

Materials Needed by Students for Completion

- Poster board or large white paper
- Recording software or application (for commercials)
- Charles's Law Cube template
- Large blank lined index cards (for instruction cards)
- Coat hangers (for mobiles)
- String (for mobiles)
- Blank index cards (for mobiles)
- Graph paper or Internet access (for WebQuests)
- Method for recording responses to word problems

Special Notes on the Use of This Menu

- This menu is a product and problem menu; it asks students to not only create products to demonstrate their knowledge but also answer one or more higher level problems. When introducing this menu, teachers will need to have already determined how they would like these problems completed and recorded for grading. Remember, this is the opportunity to hold high standards when it comes to showing work and defending answers!
- This menu gives students the opportunity to create a commercial. The grading and sharing of these products can often be facilitated by

having students prerecord their product using whatever technology is most convenient for the teacher. This allows the teacher to decide when it will be shown as well as keeps the presentation to its intended length. If recording options are limited, this activity can be modified by allowing students to act out the product (like a play) in front of the class.

- This menu gives students the opportunity to facilitate a class game. The expectation is that all students in the classroom will play an active role in the game. This may mean that students may need some additional space and time for their game. This can take a significant amount of time and organization. It can save time if all of the students who choose to present their game can sign up for a designated day and time that is determined when the menu is distributed.

- This menu allows students to create a WebQuest. There are multiple versions and templates for WebQuests available on the Internet. It is your decision whether you would like to specify a format or if you will allow students to create one of their own choosing.

Time Frame

- 2–3 weeks—Students are given their menu as the unit is started, and the guidelines and point expectations on the back of the menu are discussed. As lessons are taught throughout the unit, students and the teacher can refer back to the options associated with that topic (or column). The teacher will go over all of the options for the topic being covered and have students place checkmarks in the boxes next to the activities they are most interested in completing. As teaching continues over the next 2–3 weeks, activities are discussed, chosen, and submitted for grading.

- 1 week—At the beginning of the unit, the teacher chooses an activity from each area he or she feels would be most valuable for students. Stations can be set up in the classroom or one of the teacher-selected activities could be provided each day for completion. These activities are available for student choice throughout the week as regular instruction takes place.

- 1–2 days—The teacher chooses an activity from an objective to use with the entire class during that lesson time.

Suggested Forms

- All-purpose rubric
- Proposal form for point-based products

Answers to Menu Problems

Problem 1: A gas with a volume of 13 L at a pressure of 142 kPa can change to a volume of 11 L. What is the pressure in the container if the temperature remains constant?

$$P_1V_1 = P_2V_2$$

$$\left(142\ \text{kPa}\right)\left(13\ \text{L}\right) = \left(x\right)\left(11\text{L}\right)$$

$$\frac{1846\ \text{kPa} \cdot \text{L}}{11\ \text{L}} = \frac{11\ \text{L}\left(x\right)}{11\ \text{L}}$$

$$168\ \text{kPa} = x$$

The pressure of the container is 168 kPa.

Problem 2: A container containing 1.35 moles of a gas is collected at 27 °C and then allowed to expand to 40.0 L. What must the new temperature (°C) be in order to maintain the same pressure?

$$\frac{V_1}{T_1} = \frac{V_2}{T_2}$$

$$V_1 = 1.35\ \text{mol} \cdot \frac{22.4\ \text{L}}{1\ \text{mol}} = 30.2\ \text{L} \qquad T_1 = 27\ °\text{C} + 273\ °\text{C} = 300\ °\text{K}$$

$$V_2 = 40.0\ \text{L} \qquad T_2 = x$$

$$\frac{30.2\ \text{L}}{300\ °\text{K}} = \frac{40.0\ \text{L}}{x}$$

$$\left(30.2\ \text{L}\right)\left(x\right) = \left(40.0\ \text{L}\right)\left(300\ °\text{K}\right)$$

$$\frac{30.2\ \text{L}\left(x\right)}{30.2\ \text{L}} = \frac{12{,}000\ \text{L}\ °\text{K}}{30.2\ \text{L}}$$

$$x = 397 \, °K$$

$$397 \, °K - 273 \, °K = 124 \, °C$$

Problem 3: If 46.2 grams of O_2 has a volume of 20 L at the same temperature and pressure, what would be the volume of 38.3 grams of O_2?

$$\frac{V_1}{n_1} = \frac{V_2}{n_2}$$

$$V_1 = 20 \, L \quad V_2 = x$$

$$n_1 = 46.2 \, g \, O_2 \cdot \frac{1 \, mol \, O_2}{32 \, g \, O_2} = 1.44 \, mol \, O_2 \quad n_2 = 38.3 \, g \, O_2 \cdot \frac{1 \, mol \, O_2}{32 \, g \, O_2} = 1.20 \, mol \, O_2$$

$$\frac{20 \, L}{1.44 \, mol} = \frac{x}{1.20 \, mol}$$

$$\left(20 \, L\right)\left(1.2 \, mol\right) = \left(1.44 \, mol\right)\left(x\right)$$

$$\frac{24 \, L \, mol}{1.44 \, mol} = \frac{1.44 \, mol \left(x\right)}{1.44 \, mol}$$

$$16.7 \, L = x$$

Problem 4: A gas is heated from 205 °K to 315 °K, and the volume is increased from 13.3 L to 21.4 L. If the original pressure was 562 torr, what would the final pressure be?

$$\frac{P_1 V_1}{T_1} = \frac{P_2 V_2}{T_2}$$

$$P_1 = 562 \, torr \quad P_2 = x$$

$$V_1 = 13.3 \, L \quad V_2 = 21.4 \, L$$

$$T_1 = 205\ ^\circ K \quad T_2 = 315\ ^\circ K$$

$$\frac{(562\ \text{torr})(13.3\ \text{L})}{205\ ^\circ K} = \frac{(x)(21.4\ \text{L})}{315\ ^\circ K}$$

$$(562\ \text{torr})(13.3\ \text{L})(315\ ^\circ K) = (x)(21.4\ \text{L})(205\ ^\circ K)$$

$$\frac{2{,}354{,}499\ \text{torr L}\ ^\circ K}{4{,}387\ \text{L}\ ^\circ K} = \frac{4{,}387\ \text{L}\ ^\circ K(x)}{4{,}387\ \text{L}\ ^\circ K}$$

$$537\ \text{torr} = x$$

Problem 5: If you have 52.6 L of water vapor at a pressure of 742 torr and at a temperature of 56 °C, what is the volume of the container that the vapor is in?

$$PV = nrt$$

$$P = 742\ \text{torr} \quad V = x$$

$$n = 52.6\ \text{L} \cdot \frac{1\ \text{mol H}_2\text{O}}{22.4\text{L H}_2\text{O}} = 2.35\ \text{mol H}_2\text{O}$$

$$r = 62.364\ \frac{\text{L torr}}{\text{mol}\ ^\circ K} \qquad t = 56.0\ ^\circ C + 273\ ^\circ C = 329\ ^\circ K$$

$$(742\ \text{torr})(x) = (2.35\ \text{mol})\left(62.364\ \frac{\text{L torr}}{\text{mol}\ ^\circ K}\right)(329\ ^\circ K)$$

$$\frac{(742\ \text{torr})(x)}{(742\ \text{torr})} = \frac{48{,}217\ \text{L} \cdot \text{torr}}{742\ \text{torr}}$$

$$x = 65.0\ \text{L}$$

The volume of the container is 65.0 L.

Problem 6: If we place 30 L of O_2 and 15 L of Cl_2 into a 22 L container at a temperature of 21 °C, what will the pressure of the resulting mixture be?

$$PV = nrt$$

Oxygen:

$$P = x \quad V = 22 \text{ L}$$

$$n = 30 \text{ L } O_2 \cdot \frac{1 \text{ mol } O_2}{22.4 \text{ L } O_2} = 1.34 \text{ mol } O_2$$

$$r = .0821 \frac{\text{L} \cdot \text{atm}}{\text{K} \cdot \text{mol}} \quad t = 21 \text{ °C} + 273 \text{ °C} = 294 \text{ °K}$$

$$(x)(22 \text{ L}) = (1.34 \text{ mol})\left(.0821 \frac{\text{L} \cdot \text{atm}}{\text{K} \cdot \text{mol}}\right)(294 \text{ °K})$$

$$\frac{(22.0 \text{ L})(x)}{22 \text{ L}} = \frac{32.3 \text{ L} \cdot \text{atm}}{22 \text{ L}}$$

$$x = 1.47 \text{ atm}$$

Chlorine:

$$P = x \quad V = 22 \text{ L}$$

$$n = 15 \text{ L } Cl_2 \cdot \frac{1 \text{ mol } Cl_2}{22.4 \text{ L } Cl_2} = .67 \text{ mol } Cl_2$$

$$r = .0821 \frac{\text{L} \cdot \text{atm}}{\text{K} \cdot \text{mol}} \quad t = 21 \text{ °C} + 273 \text{ °C} = 294 \text{ °K}$$

$$(x)(22 \text{ L}) = (.67 \text{ mol})\left(.0821 \frac{\text{L} \cdot \text{atm}}{\text{K} \cdot \text{mol}}\right)(294 \text{ °K})$$

$$\frac{(22\text{ L})(x)}{22\text{ L}} = \frac{16.2\text{ L} \cdot \text{atm}}{22\text{ L}}$$

$$x = .736\text{ atm}$$

Total Pressure:

$$P_{tot} = P_O + P_{Cl}$$

$$P_{tot} = 1.47\text{ atm} + .736\text{ atm}$$

$$P_{tot} = 2.206\text{ atm}$$

The total pressure would be 2.206 atm.

Guidelines for the Gas Laws Game Show Menu

- You must choose at least one activity from each topic area.
- You may not do more than two activities in any one topic area for credit. (You are, of course, welcome to do more than two for your own investigation.)
- Grading will be ongoing, so turn in products as you complete them.
- All free-choice proposals must be turned in and approved *prior* to working on the free choice.
- You must earn **150** points for a 100%. You may earn extra credit up to _____ points.
- You must show your teacher your plan for completion by: _____ .

Name:_____ Date:_____

Gas Laws

Boyle's Law	Charles's Law	Avogadro's Law	Combined Gas Law	Ideal Gas Law	Dalton's Law of Partial Pressure	Points for Each Level
☐ Record a video of you doing two demonstrations that illustrate Boyle's law. (15 pts.)	☐ Fold a product cube that has everyday examples of Charles's law in the world around us. (10 pts.)	☐ Create an instruction card for identifying and solving Avogadro's law problems. (10 pts.)	☐ Develop a poster to show how the combined gas law truly is a combination of all of the other gas laws. (15 pts.)	☐ Assemble an ideal gas laws mobile that shows each of the variables, their meanings, and their units. (10 pts.)	☐ Write three facts and fib about when (or how) to use Dalton's law of partial pressure. (15 pts.)	**10–15 points**
☐ **Problem 1:** A gas with a volume of 13 L at a pressure of 142 kPa can change to a volume of 11 L. What is the pressure in the container if the temperature remains constant? (20 pts.)	☐ **Problem 2:** A container containing 1.35 moles of a gas is collected at 27 °C and then allowed to expand to 40.0 L. What must the new temperature (°C) be in order to maintain the same pressure? (25 pts.)	☐ **Problem 3:** If 46.2 grams of O_2 has a volume of 20 L at the same temperature and pressure, what would be the volume of 38.3 grams of O_2? (25 pts.)	☐ **Problem 4:** A gas is heated from 205 °K to 315 °K, and the volume is increased from 13.3 L to 21.4 L. If the original pressure was 562 torr, what would the final pressure be? (20 pts.)	☐ **Problem 5:** If you have 52.6 L of water vapor at a pressure of 742 torr and at a temperature of 56 °C, what is the volume of the container that the vapor is in? (25 pts.)	☐ **Problem 6:** If we place 30 L of O_2 and 15 L of Cl_2 in a 22 L container at a temperature of 21° C, what will the pressure of the resulting mixture be? (25 pts.)	**20–25 points**
☐ Design a social media profile for Boyle's law. Be creative in how you represent its personality. (30 pts.)	☐ Record a speech in which a politician uses Charles's law concepts to explain a current event in our country. (30 pts.)	☐ Record a commercial in which a misunderstanding of Avogadro's law has funny results. (30 pts.)	☐ Prepare a class game that will allow your classmates to practice their skills in solving combined gas law problems. (30 pts.)	☐ Develop an original WebQuest about the ideal gas law, including real-world applications and calculations. (30 pts.)	☐ Propose a classroom model that could be used to demonstrate Dalton's law of partial pressure. (30 pts.)	**30 points**
Free Choice (prior approval) (10–30 pts.)	**Free Choice** (prior approval) (10–30 pts.)	**Free Choice** (prior approval) (10–30 pts.)	**Free Choice** (prior approval) (10–30 pts.)	**Free Choice** (prior approval) (10–30 pts.)	**Free Choice** (prior approval) (10–30 pts.)	**10–30 points**
Total:	**Total:**	**Total:**	**Total:**	**Total:**	**Total:**	**Total Grade:**

Charles's Law Cube

Fold a product cube that has everyday examples of Charles's Law in the world around us.

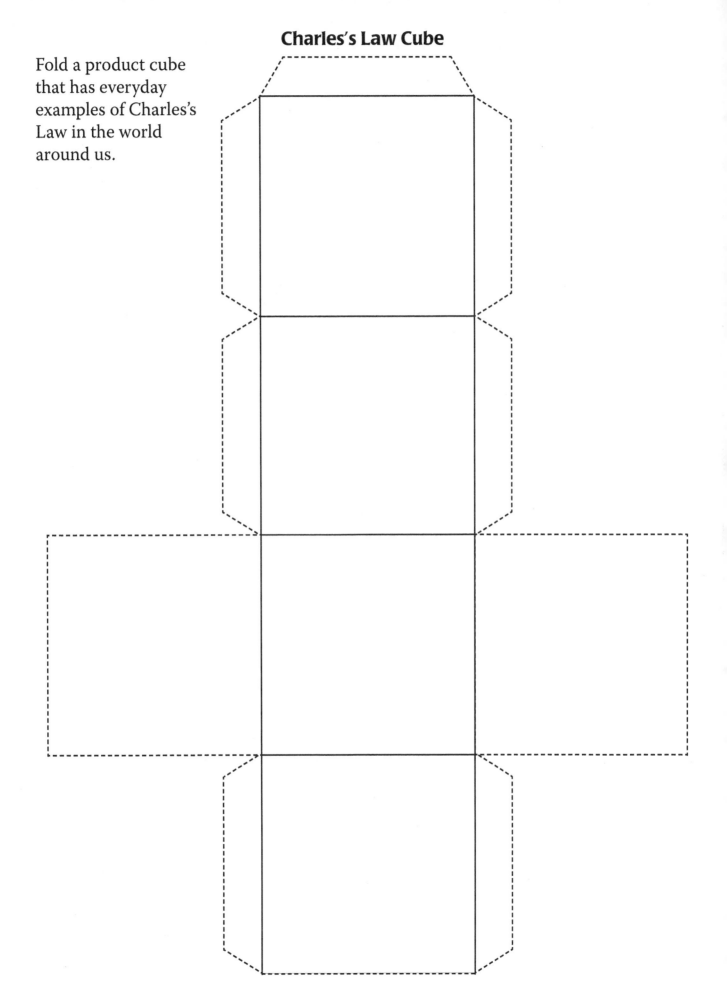

Charles's Law Cube

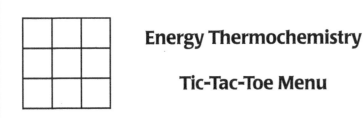

Energy Thermochemistry

Tic-Tac-Toe Menu

Objectives Covered Through This Menu and These Activities

- Students will be able to describe energy and its forms, including kinetic, potential, chemical, and thermal energies.
- Students will be able to describe the law of conservation of energy and the processes of heat transfer in terms of calorimetry.
- Students will be able to perform calculations involving heat, mass, temperature change, and specific heat.
- Students will express and manipulate chemical quantities using chemical conventions and mathematical procedures.
- Students will communicate valid conclusions supported by data.

Materials Needed by Students for Completion

- Poster board or large white paper
- Blank index cards (for card sorts)
- Recording software or application (for videos)
- Recycled materials (for museum exhibits)
- Method for recording responses to word problems

Special Notes on the Use of This Menu

- This menu is a product and problem menu; it asks students to not only create products to demonstrate their knowledge but also answer one or more higher level word problems. It is set up in such a way that students will have to complete at least one of the word problems. When introducing this menu, teachers will need to have already determined how they would like these problems completed and recorded for grading. Remember, this is the opportunity to hold high standards when it comes to showing work and defending answers!
- This menu gives students the opportunity to create a video. The grading and sharing of these products can often be facilitated by having students prerecord their product using whatever technology is most convenient for the teacher. This allows the teacher to decide when it will be shown as well as keeps the presentation to its intended length. If recording options are limited, this activity can be modified by allowing students to act out the product (like a play) in front of the class.

- This menu asks students to use recycled materials to create their museum exhibit. This does not mean only plastic and paper; instead, students should focus on using materials in new ways. It works well if a box is started for "recycled" contributions at the beginning of the school year. That way, students always have access to these types of materials.

Time Frame

- 2–3 weeks—Students are given the menu as the unit is started. The teacher will go over all of the options for that content and have students place checkmarks in the boxes that represent the activities they are most interested in completing. As students choose activities, they should complete a column or a row. When students complete this pattern, they have completed one activity from each content area, learning style, or level of Bloom's revised taxonomy, depending on the design of the menu. As the teacher presents lessons throughout the week, he or she should refer back to the menu options associated with that content.
- 1 week—At the start of the unit, the teacher chooses the three activities he or she feels are most valuable for students. Stations can be set up in the classroom. These three activities are available for student choice throughout the week as regular instruction takes place.
- 1–2 days—The teacher chooses an activity from the menu to use with the entire class.

Suggested Forms

- All-purpose rubric
- Free-choice proposal form

Answers to Menu Problems

Problem 1: A teacher filled a cup with about 100 g of ice from the freezer (set at 28 °F). He forgot to fill the cup in his hurry to class so he left it on his desk. Almost 3 hours later, it had come to room temperature (74 °F). Draw a phase change diagram for this change. Was energy lost or gained? How much?

Phase change diagram:

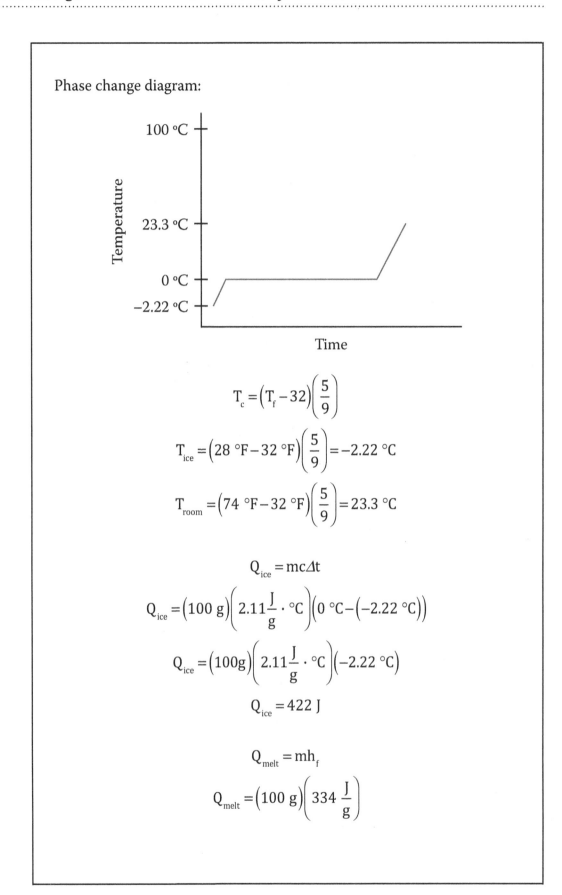

$$T_c = \left(T_f - 32\right)\left(\frac{5}{9}\right)$$

$$T_{ice} = \left(28\ °F - 32\ °F\right)\left(\frac{5}{9}\right) = -2.22\ °C$$

$$T_{room} = \left(74\ °F - 32\ °F\right)\left(\frac{5}{9}\right) = 23.3\ °C$$

$$Q_{ice} = mc\Delta t$$

$$Q_{ice} = \left(100\ g\right)\left(2.11\frac{J}{g} \cdot °C\right)\left(0\ °C - \left(-2.22\ °C\right)\right)$$

$$Q_{ice} = \left(100g\right)\left(2.11\frac{J}{g} \cdot °C\right)\left(-2.22\ °C\right)$$

$$Q_{ice} = 422\ J$$

$$Q_{melt} = mh_f$$

$$Q_{melt} = \left(100\ g\right)\left(334\ \frac{J}{g}\right)$$

$$Q_{melt} = 33{,}400 \text{ J}$$

$$Q_{liquid} = mc\Delta t$$

$$Q_{liquid} = (100 \text{ g})\left(4.18 \ \frac{\text{J}}{\text{g} \, °\text{C}}\right)(23.3 \, °\text{C} - 0 \, °\text{C})$$

$$Q_{liquid} = (100 \text{ g})\left(4.18 \frac{\text{J}}{\text{g} \, °\text{C}}\right)(23.3 \, °\text{C})$$

$$Q_{liquid} = 9{,}739.4 \text{ J}$$

$$Q_{total} = Q_{ice} + Q_{melt} + Q_{liquid}$$

$$Q_{total} = 422 \text{ J} + 34{,}000 \text{ J} + 9{,}739.4 \text{ J}$$

$$Q_{total} = 44{,}161.4 \text{ J}$$

44,161.4 J or 44.2 KJ of energy were gained.

Problem 2: You were given a 52 g sample of copper at room temperature (74 °F). If you added 3,548 J of energy to the copper, what would its final temperature be? Would it still be a solid? Draw a phase change diagram to accompany your work.

Phase change diagram:

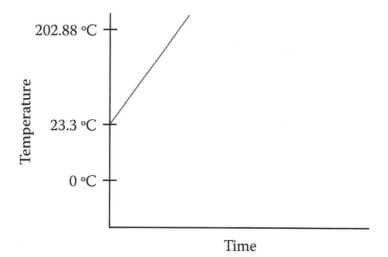

$$T_c = \left(T_f - 32\right)\left(\frac{5}{9}\right)$$

$$T_c = \left(74 \ ^\circ F\right) - 32\left(\frac{5}{9}\right) = 23.33 \ ^\circ C$$

$$Q = mc\varDelta t \qquad \varDelta t = T_f - T_c$$

$$3{,}548 \ J = \left(52 \ g\right)\left(.38 \ \frac{J}{g \ ^\circ C}\right)\left(T_f - 23.33 \ ^\circ C\right)$$

$$\frac{3{,}548 \ J}{19.76 \ \frac{J}{^\circ C}} = \frac{19.76 \ \frac{J}{^\circ C}}{19.76 \ \frac{J}{^\circ C}}\left(T_f - 23.33 \ ^\circ C\right)$$

$$179.55 \ ^\circ C \ = \quad T_f - 23.33 \ ^\circ C$$

$$+ \ 23.33 \ ^\circ C \quad + \ 23.33 \ ^\circ C$$

$$202.88 \ ^\circ C = T_f$$

Because copper melts at 1,085 °C, the copper remains a solid.

Problem 3: After drawing a phase diagram for water, calculate the number of kilojoules needed to change 32 g of ice at −4 °C into water vapor at 106 °C.

Phase change diagram:

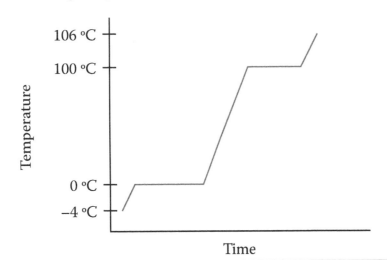

$$Q = mc\Delta t \qquad Hf_{water} = 334\frac{J}{g}$$

$$C_{ice} = 2.11\frac{J}{g\,^\circ C} \qquad Hv_{water} = 2{,}230\frac{J}{g}$$

$$C_{water} = 4.18\frac{J}{g\,^\circ C} \qquad C_{vapor} = 2\frac{J}{g\,^\circ C}$$

$$1\ KJ = 1{,}000\ J$$

$$Q_{ice} = (32g)\left(2.11\frac{J}{g\,^\circ C}\right)(4\,^\circ C) = 270.1\ J$$

$$Q_{melt} = (32g)\left(334\frac{J}{g}\right) = 10{,}688\ J$$

$$Q_{water} = (32g)\left(4.18\frac{J}{g\,^\circ C}\right)(100\,^\circ C) = 13{,}376\ J$$

$$Q_{boil} = (32g)\left(2{,}230\frac{J}{g}\right) = 71{,}360\ J$$

$$Q_{vapor} = (32g)\left(2\frac{J}{g\,^\circ C}\right)(6\,^\circ C) = 384\ J$$

$$Q_{total} = Q_{ice} + Q_{melt} + Q_{water} + Q_{boil} + Q_{vapor}$$

$$Q_{total} = 270.1\ J + 10{,}688\ J + 13{,}376\ J + 71{,}360\ J + 384\ J$$

$$Q_{total} = 96{,}078.1\ J \cdot \frac{1\ KJ}{1{,}000\ J} = 96.08\ KJ$$

Energy Thermochemistry

Directions: Check the boxes you plan to complete. They should form a tic-tac-toe across or down. All products are due by: _____ .

☐ *Understanding Specific Heat*	☐ *Problem 1*	☐ *Law of Conservation of Energy*
Design a card sort (with answer key) with pictures of items on one side of each card and their specific heat values on the other so that others could use the cards to predict specific heats from highest to lowest values.	A teacher filled a cup with about 100 g of ice from the freezer (set at 28 °F). He forgot to fill the cup in his hurry to class so he left it on his desk. Almost 3 hours later, it had come to room temperature (74 °F). Draw a phase change diagram for this change. Was energy lost or gained? How much?	Build an interactive museum exhibit that could teach visitors about how the law of conservation of energy impacts our lives.
☐ *Law of Conservation of Energy*	☐ **Free Choice: Understanding Specific Heat**	☐ *Problem 2*
Although the law of conservation of energy does not apply to people, many wish it could. Write a play or skit about two different fictitious people who are living the law of conservation of energy.	(Fill out your proposal form before beginning the free choice!)	You were given a 52 g sample of copper at room temperature (74 °F). If you added 3,548 J of energy to the copper, what would its final temperature be? Would it still be a solid? Draw a phase change diagram to accompany your work.
☐ *Problem 3*	☐ *Law of Conservation of Energy*	☐ *Understanding Specific Heat*
After drawing a phase diagram for water, calculate the number of kilojoules needed to change 32 g of ice at −4 °C into water vapor at 106 °C.	Record an original video that introduces watchers to everyday examples of the law of conservation of energy.	Develop an advertisement for a new product whose most helpful feature is it high specific heat.

CHAPTER 8

Bonding

 DOI: 10.4324/9781003234357-10

Covalent and Ionic Compounds

Three-Topic List Menu

Objectives Covered Through This Menu and These Activities

- Students will be able to name ionic compounds containing main group or transition metals, and covalent compounds, using International Union of Pure and Applied Chemistry (IUPAC) nomenclature rules.
- Students will be able to write the chemical formulas of ionic compounds containing representative elements, transition metals and common polyatomic ions, and covalent compounds.
- Students will communicate valid conclusions supported by data.

Materials Needed by Students for Completion

- Poster board or large white paper
- Recording software or application (for documentaries and videos)
- Recycled materials (for models, museum exhibits)
- Blank index cards (for card sorts)
- Large blank lined index cards (for instruction cards)
- Creating Compounds Cube template

Special Notes on the Use of This Menu

- This menu gives students the opportunity to create a video and a documentary. The grading and sharing of these products can often be facilitated by having students prerecord their product using whatever technology is most convenient for the teacher. This allows the teacher to decide when it will be shown as well as keeps the presentation to its intended length. If recording options are limited, this activity can be modified by allowing students to act out the product (like a play) in front of the class.
- This menu asks students to use recycled materials to create their museum exhibits and models. This does not mean only plastic and paper; instead, students should focus on using materials in new ways. It works well if a box is started for "recycled" contributions at the beginning of the school year. That way, students always have access to these types of materials.
- This menu gives students the opportunity to facilitate a class game. The expectation is that all students in the classroom will play an active

role in the game. This may mean that students need some additional space and time for their game. This can take a significant amount of time and organization. It can save time if all of the students who choose to present their game can sign up for a designated day and time that is determined when the menu is distributed.

Time Frame

- 1–2 weeks—Students are given the menu as the unit is started, and the guidelines and point expectations are discussed. Students usually will need to earn 100 points for 100%, although there is an opportunity for extra credit if the teacher would like to use another target number. Because this menu covers one topic in depth, the teacher will go over all of the options for the topic being covered and have students place checkmarks in the boxes next to the activities they are most interested in completing. Teachers will need to set aside a few moments to sign the agreement at the bottom of the page with each student. As instruction continues, activities are completed by students and submitted to the teacher for grading.
- 1–2 days—The teacher chooses an activity or product from an objective to use with the entire class during that lesson time.

Suggested Forms

- All-purpose rubric
- Proposal form for point-based products

Name:_____ Date:_____

Covalent and Ionic Compounds

Guidelines:
1. You may complete as many of the activities listed as you wish within the time period.
2. You may choose any combination of activities, but **must** complete at least one activity from each topic area.
3. Your goal is 100 points. (This is a grade of 100/100.) You may earn up to _____ points extra credit.
4. You may be as creative as you like within the guidelines listed below.
5. You must show your plan to your teacher by _____ .
6. Activities may be turned in at any time during the working time period. They will be graded and recorded on this sheet as you continue to work, so keep it safe!

Topic	Plan to Do	Activity to Complete	Point Value	Date Completed	Points Earned
Ionic and Covalent Compounds		Make a poster that shows how to tell the difference between ionic and covalent compounds.	10		
		Design a card sort in which players sort chemical compounds into two groups: *Ionic* and *Covalent.* Include cards with compound names as well as correct chemical formulas.	15		
		Assemble two cubes with elements on each one so that when each cube is rolled, an ionic or covalent compound is formed. Include an answer key of all of the different compounds that could be created using the cubes.	25		
		You have been given the task to create a museum exhibit in a box for a traveling chemistry museum. Your topic is *Ionic and Covalent Compounds—All Around Us.* Your exhibit should include chemical formulas and names.	30		
Ionic Compounds		Write an instruction card to explain how to write the names of ionic compounds. Include polyatomic ions and roman numerals.	10		
		Draw a picture dictionary that shows drawings of at least 10 ionic compounds. Record the name and chemical formula for each compound on its page.	15		
		Record a video that explains why roman numerals are necessary when writing the name of certain compounds. Include multiple examples of compounds that require a roman numeral and those that do not.	20		
		Build a model that could be used to demonstrate how ionic compounds are created from ions. Your model should include names of the compounds as well as polyatomic ions.	25		
Covalent Compounds		Create a flipbook to help review the different prefixes used in naming covalent compounds.	10		
		Prepare a class game that has players naming covalent compounds when given a formula or writing formulas when given a name.	15		
		Create an imaginative riddle- or puzzle-based worksheet to help others practice writing and naming covalent compounds.	20		
		Record a documentary that shares the potential dangers of dihydrogen monoxide.	25		
Any		**Free Choice:** Submit your free choice proposal form for a product of your choice.			
		Total number of points you are planning to earn.		**Total points earned:**	

I am planning to complete _____ activities that could earn up to a total of _____ points.

Teacher's initials _____ Student's signature _____

Creating Compounds Cube

Assemble two cubes with elements on each one so that when each cube is rolled, an ionic or covalent compound is formed. Include an answer key of all of the different compounds that could be created using the cubes.

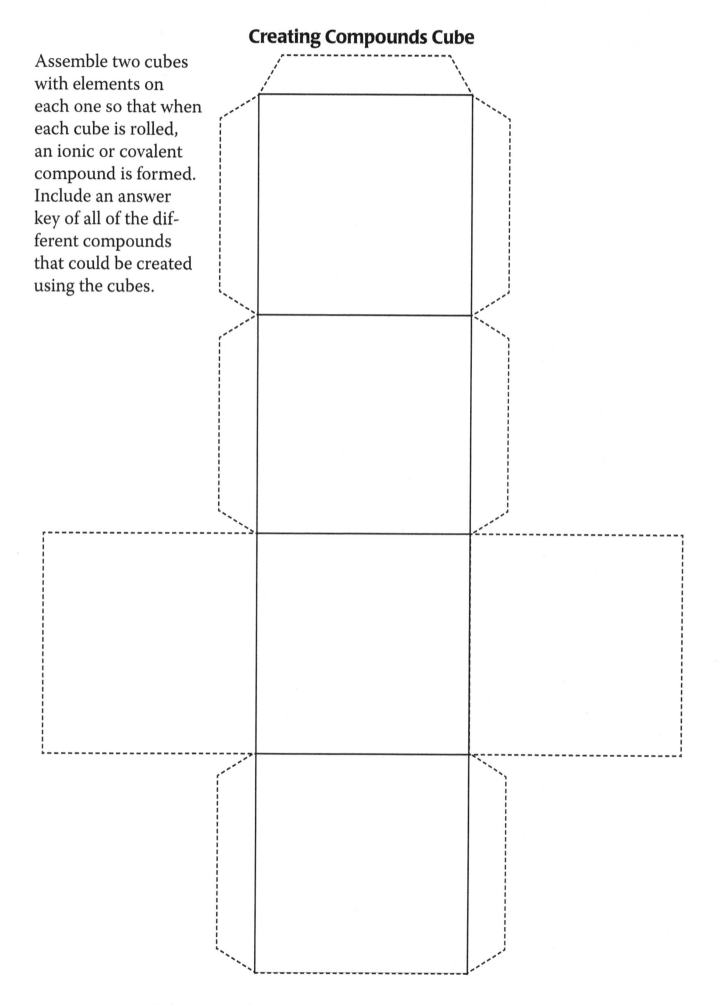

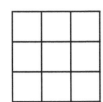

Bonding

Tic-Tac-Toe Menu

Objectives Covered Through This Menu and These Activities
- Students will be able to construct electron dot formulas to illustrate ionic and covalent bonds.
- Students will communicate valid conclusions supported by data.

Materials Needed by Students for Completion
- Poster board or large white paper
- Blank index cards (for trading cards)
- Recording software or application (for videos)
- Materials for bulletin board display
- Method for recording responses to word problems

Special Notes on the Use of This Menu
- This menu gives students the opportunity to create a video. The grading and sharing of these products can often be facilitated by having students prerecord their product using whatever technology is most convenient for the teacher. This allows the teacher to decide when it will be shown as well as keeps the presentation to its intended length. If recording options are limited, this activity can be modified by allowing students to act out the product (like a play) in front of the class.
- This menu gives students the opportunity to facilitate a class model. The expectation is that all students in the classroom will play an active role in the model. This may mean that students need some additional space for their model.
- This menu allows students to create a bulletin board display. Some classrooms may only have one bulletin board, so the teacher can divide the board into sections, or additional classroom wall or hall space can be sectioned off for the creation of these displays. Students can plan their display based on the amount of space they are assigned.

Time Frame
- 2–3 weeks—Students are given the menu as the unit is started. The teacher will go over all of the options for that content and have students place checkmarks in the boxes that represent the activities they

are most interested in completing. As students choose activities, they should complete a column or a row. When students complete this pattern, they have completed one activity from each content area, learning style, or level of Bloom's revised taxonomy, depending on the design of the menu. As the teacher presents lessons throughout the week, he or she should refer back to the menu options associated with that content.

- 1 week—At the start of the unit, the teacher chooses the three activities he or she feels are most valuable for students. Stations can be set up in the classroom. These three activities are available for student choice throughout the week as regular instruction takes place.
- 1–2 days—The teacher chooses an activity from the menu to use with the entire class.

Suggested Forms

- All-purpose rubric
- Free-choice proposal form

Name:_____ Date:_____

Bonding

Directions: Check the boxes you plan to complete. They should form a tic-tac-toe across or down. All products are due by: _____ .

☐ *Ionic Bonds* Make a folded quiz book to quiz your classmates on drawing ionic bonds using electron dot formulas.	☐ *Illustrating Bonding* Design a bulletin board display to illustrate electron dot formulas for both ionic and covalent compounds.	☐ *Covalent Bonding* Prepare a You Be the Covalent Electron presentation in which you come to class and discuss your role in a covalent bond.
☐ *Covalent Bonding* Create a set of trading cards for elements that typically participate in covalent bonding. Be sure each card includes examples of typical covalent bonds each element forms.	☐ **Free Choice: Ionic Bonds** (Fill out your proposal form before beginning the free choice!)	☐ *Illustrating Bonding* Write a children's book about two electrons, one that participates in a covalent bond and one that participates in an ionic bond. All illustrations should be chemically correct.
☐ *Illustrating Bonding* Record a video that shows how different types of bonding take place. Use electron dot formulas as part of your video.	☐ *Covalent Bonding* Draw a cartoon that shows how electrons are impacted in a covalent bond.	☐ *Ionic Bonds* Create a classroom model in which your classmates become electron dot formulas for an ionic bond with at least three ions.

Molecular Structure

20-50-80 Menu

Objectives Covered Through This Menu and These Activities

- Students will be able to classify molecular structure for molecules' different electron pair geometries as explained by Valence Shell Electron Pair Repulsion (VSEPR) theory.
- Students will communicate valid conclusions supported by data.
- Students will critique scientific explanations and evaluate the impact of research on scientific thought.

Materials Needed by Students for Completion

- Poster board or large white paper
- Microsoft PowerPoint or other slideshow software
- Coat hangers (for mobiles)
- String (for mobiles)
- Blank index cards (for mobiles, and trading cards)
- Recording software or application (for how-to videos)

Special Notes on the Use of This Menu

- This menu gives students the opportunity to create a how-to video. The grading and sharing of these products can often be facilitated by having students prerecord their product using whatever technology is most convenient for the teacher. This allows the teacher to decide when it will be shown as well as keeps the presentation to its intended length. If recording options are limited, this activity can be modified by allowing students to act out the product (like a play) in front of the class.
- This menu gives students the opportunity to teach a concept. This can take a significant amount of time and organization. It can save time if the students who choose to do a lesson can sign up for a designated day and time that is determined when the menu is distributed.

Time Frame

- 1–2 weeks—Students are given a menu as the unit is started, and the teacher discusses all of the product options on the menu. As the different options are discussed, students will choose the activities they are most interested in completing so that they meet their goal of 100 points. As the lessons progress through the week(s), the teacher and students refer back to the menu options associated with the content being taught.

- 1–2 days—The teacher chooses an activity or product from the menu to use with the entire class.

Suggested Forms

- All-purpose rubric
- Student-taught lesson rubric
- Proposal form for point-based projects

Name:_____ Date:_____

Molecular Structure

Directions: Choose at least two activities from the menu below. The activities must total 100 points. Place a checkmark next to each box to show which activities you will complete. All activities must be completed by _____ .

---

20 Points

❐ Assemble a mobile with examples of each of the types of molecular structures we are discussing in class.

❐ Draw a picture dictionary for each of the molecular structures we are studying.

---

50 Points

❐ Record a how-to video to teach your classmates about drawing the molecular structure for various polar and nonpolar compounds.

❐ Create a set of trading cards for each of the molecular structures we are discussing. Include how/why each is formed, including bond angles and polarity.

❐ Make a Venn diagram to compare a polar and nonpolar molecular structures.

❐ **Free choice on molecular structures**—Prepare a proposal form and submit it to your teacher for approval.

---

80 Points

❐ Investigate at least two different molecular structures we did not discuss in class. Prepare a class lesson to teach your classmates about the electron dot formulas, bond angles, and polarity associated with each structure.

❐ Research the mathematics behind the bond angles in different molecular structures. Develop a PowerPoint (or using other similar software) to explain the mathematical reasoning for each bond angle.

CHAPTER 9

Solutions

 DOI: 10.4324/9781003234357-11

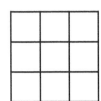

Solubility

Tic-Tac-Toe Menu

Objectives Covered Through This Menu and These Activities
- Students will be able to distinguish between unsaturated, saturated, and supersaturated solutions.
- Students will investigate factors that influence solid and gas solubilities and rates of dissolution, such as temperature, agitation, and surface area.
- Students will plan and implement procedures.
- Students will collect data and make measurements with accuracy and precision.
- Students will express and manipulate chemical quantities using chemical conventions and mathematical procedures.
- Students will communicate valid conclusions supported by data.

Materials Needed by Students for Completion
- Poster board or large white paper
- Microsoft PowerPoint or other slideshow software
- Internet access (for WebQuests)
- Materials for bulletin board display
- Method for recording responses to word problems

Special Notes on the Use of This Menu
- This menu is a product and problem menu; it asks students to not only create products to demonstrate their knowledge but also answer one or more higher level word problems. It is set up in such a way that students will have to complete at least one of the word problems. When introducing this menu, teachers will need to have already determined how they would like these problems completed and recorded for grading. Remember, this is the opportunity to hold high standards when it comes to showing work and defending answers!
- This menu allows students to create a bulletin board display. Some classrooms may only have one bulletin board, so the teacher can divide the board into sections, or additional classroom wall or hall space can be sectioned off for the creation of these displays. Students can plan their display based on the amount of space they are assigned.

- This menu allows students to create a WebQuest. There are multiple versions and templates for WebQuests available on the Internet. It is your decision whether you would like to specify a format or if you will allow students to create one of their own choosing.

Time Frame

- 2–3 weeks—Students are given the menu as the unit is started. The teacher will go over all of the options for that content and have students place checkmarks in the boxes that represent the activities they are most interested in completing. As students choose activities, they should complete a column or a row. When students complete this pattern, they have completed one activity from each content area, learning style, or level of Bloom's revised taxonomy, depending on the design of the menu. As the teacher presents lessons throughout the week, he or she should refer back to the menu options associated with that content.
- 1 week—At the start of the unit, the teacher chooses the three activities he or she feels are most valuable for students. Stations can be set up in the classroom. These three activities are available for student choice throughout the week as regular instruction takes place.
- 1–2 days—The teacher chooses an activity from the menu to use with the entire class.

Suggested Forms

- All-purpose rubric
- Student-Created Experiment Rubric
- Free-choice proposal form
- Solubility Curve

Answers to Menu Problems

Problem 1: Given 23 g of potassium nitrate per 25 g of water, what temperature should create a saturated solution?

$$\frac{23 \text{ g } KNO_3}{25 \text{ g } H_2O} = \frac{x \text{ g } KNO_3}{100 \text{ g } H_2O}$$

$$\frac{2{,}300 \text{ g } KNO_3 \cdot H_2O}{25 \text{ g } H_2O} = 92 \text{ g } KNO_3$$

Knowing we have 92 grams of KNO_3 per 100 grams of water, we can use the solubility curve. The temperature would be approximately 57 °C.

Problem 2: You have been given 42 g of a mystery solid. When placed in 100 g of water and heated to approximately 29 °C, it appears to create a saturated solution. State your conclusions about the identity of the substance.

This is a trick question, as four of the curves (NH_3, NH_4Cl, KNO_3, and NaCl) cross in this area. The students should realize they will not know the identity using just the curves. Given that the substance is a solid, NH_3 is not a possible answer. Therefore, without further testing, we can only conclude that the substance could be NH_4Cl, KNO_3, or NaCl.

Problem 3: You are given 80 g of sodium nitrate in 200 g of water at 10 °C. You would like to create a saturated solution. How many grams of solute (if any) would you have to add or remove to do so? Explain your answer.

According to the solubility curve for sodium nitrate ($NaNO_3$), at 10 °C, a saturated solution is created by 80 g of sodium nitrate ($NaNO_3$) in 100 g of water. Because we are using 200 g of water in our solution, a saturated solution is created with 160 g. Because the amount of solvent has doubled, the amount of solute must double as well. So, in order to create a saturated solution, we would need to add 80 more grams of sodium nitrate ($NaNO_3$).

Name:_____ Date:_____

Solubility

Directions: Check the boxes you plan to complete. They should form a tic-tac-toe across or down. All products are due by: _____ .

☐ *Investigating Solubility Factors* Design an original science experiment to test different factors that influence rates of dissolution.	☐ *Solubility Curves* Consider the trends of solubility curves. Prepare a bulletin board display that provides insight into the properties of the substances that demonstrate each trend.	☐ *Problem 1* Given 23 g of potassium nitrate per 25 g of water, what temperature should create a saturated solution?
☐ *Problem 2* You have been given 42 g of a mystery solid. When placed in 100 g of water and heated to approximately 29 °C, it appears to create a saturated solution. State your conclusions about the identity of the substance.	☐ **Free Choice: Investigating Solubility Factors** (Fill out your proposal form before beginning the free choice!)	☐ *Solubility Curves* Investigate at least eight other substances not included on your current solubility graph that represent different types of matter. On a poster, design a new solubility graph for these substances.
☐ *Solubility Curves* Create an *original* quiz that asks questions about solubility curves. Focus your quiz on the unusual aspects of the curves and be tricky!	☐ *Problem 3* You are given 80 g of sodium nitrate in 200 g of water at 10 °C. You would like to create a saturated solution. How many grams of solute (if any) would you have to add or remove to do so? Explain your answer.	☐ *Investigating Solubility Factors* Develop a WebQuest that allows questors to observe (and interact with) different experiments that show factors that influence rates of dissolution.

Solubility Curve

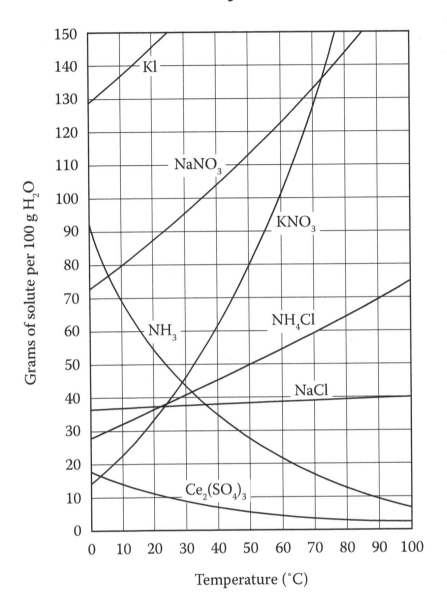

© Taylor & Francis • *Differentiating Instruction With Menus: Chemistry • Grades 9–12*

Molarity

Two-Topic List Menu

Objectives Covered Through This Menu and These Activities
- Students will be able to understand the concept of molarity.
- Students will be able to calculate the concentration of solutions in units of molarity.
- Students will express and manipulate chemical quantities using chemical conventions and mathematical procedures.
- Students will communicate valid conclusions supported by data.

Materials Needed by Students for Completion
- Poster board or large white paper
- Blank index cards (for card sorts)
- Magazines (for collages)
- Large blank lined index cards (for instruction cards)

Special Notes on the Use of This Menu
- This menu is a product and problem menu; it asks students to not only create products to demonstrate their knowledge but also answer one or more higher level word problems. It is set up in such a way that students will have to complete at least one of the word problems. When introducing this menu, teachers will need to have already determined how they would like these problems completed and recorded for grading. Remember, this is the opportunity to hold high standards when it comes to showing work and defending answers!
- This menu gives students the opportunity to facilitate a class model. The expectation is that all students in the classroom will play an active role in the model. This may mean that students need some additional space for their model.

Time Frame
- 1–2 weeks—Students are given the menu as the unit is started, and the guidelines and point expectations are discussed. Students usually will need to earn 100 points for 100%, although there is an opportunity for extra credit if the teacher would like to use another target number. Because this menu covers one topic in depth, the teacher

will go over all of the options for the topic being covered and have students place checkmarks in the boxes next to the activities they are most interested in completing. Teachers will need to set aside a few moments to sign the agreement at the bottom of the page with each student. As instruction continues, activities are completed by students and submitted to the teacher for grading.

- 1–2 days—The teacher chooses an activity or product from an objective to use with the entire class during that lesson time.

Suggested Forms

- All-purpose rubric
- Proposal form for point-based products

Answers to Menu Problems

Problem 1: A 2.3-liter solution contains 0.32 mol of NaCl. What is its molarity?

$$\text{Molarity}\left(M\right) = \frac{\text{moles of solute}}{\text{liters of solvent}}$$

$$M = \frac{.32 \text{ mol NaCl}}{2.3 \text{ L solvent}} = 0.14 \frac{\text{mol}}{L} \text{ or } 0.14 \text{ M}$$

Problem 2: Ocean water has a molarity of about 0.6 M. How many moles of salt would we find in 4 L?

$$0.6 \text{ M} = \frac{x}{4 \text{ L}}$$

$$\left(4 \text{ L}\right)\left(0.6 \text{ M}\right) = \frac{x}{4 \text{ L}} \cdot 4 \text{ L}$$

$$2.4 \text{ moles} = x$$

We would find 2.4 moles of salt in 4 L of ocean water.

Problem 3: If the molarity of a 355 mL can of soda is about 0.14 M, how much carbon dioxide is dissolved in the soda?

$$355 \text{ mL} \cdot \frac{1 \text{ L}}{1,000 \text{ ml}} = 0.355 \text{ L}$$

$$.14 \text{ M} = \frac{x \text{ moles}}{0.355 \text{ L}}$$

$$0.355 \text{ L} \cdot .14 \text{ M} = \frac{x \text{ moles}}{0.355 \text{ L}} \cdot 0.355 \text{ L}$$

$$0.050 \text{ moles} = x$$

There are about 0.050 moles of carbon dioxide dissolved in the soda.

Problem 4: A 3 g sugar packet ($C_{12}H_{22}O_{11}$) is emptied into a 400 mL glass of tea. What is the molarity of the solution?

Calculate moles of sugar:

$$3 \text{ g } C_{12}H_{22}O_{11} \cdot \frac{1 \text{ mol } C_{12}H_{22}O_{11}}{342.2 \text{ g } C_{12}H_{22}O_{11}} = 8.77 \times 10^{-3} \text{ mol } C_{12}H_{22}O_{11}$$

Calculate how many liters are in the tea:

$$400 \text{ mL tea} \cdot \frac{1 \text{ L}}{1,000 \text{ mL}} = .4 \text{ L of tea}$$

Calculate molarity:

$$M = \frac{8.77 \times 10^{-3} \text{ mol } C_{12}H_{22}O_{11}}{.4 \text{ L of tea}} = .02 \text{ M}$$

The molarity of the tea is 0.02 M.

Problem 5: The molarity of ocean water is about 0.6 M. Your 60-gallon saltwater fish tank is measuring at 0.52 M. How many grams of salt should you add to address this issue?

Calculate how far off the molarity is:

$$.6 \text{ M} - .52 \text{ M} = 0.08 \text{ M}$$

Calculate how many liters the tank is:

$$60 \text{ gal} \cdot \frac{3.79 \text{ L}}{1 \text{ gal}} = 227.4 \text{ L}$$

Calculate moles of salt:

$$0.08 \text{ M} = \frac{x \text{ mol NaCl}}{227.4 \text{ L water}}$$

$$227.4 \text{ L}\left(0.08 \text{ M}\right) = \frac{x \text{ mol NaCl}}{227.4 \text{ L water}}\left(227.4 \text{ L}\right)$$

$$18.19 \text{ mol} = x \text{ mol NaCl}$$

Convert moles to grams:

$$18.19 \text{ mol NaCl} \cdot \frac{58.44 \text{ g NaCl}}{1 \text{ mol NaCl}} = 1{,}063 \text{ g or } 1.063 \text{ kg}$$

You will need to add 1,063 grams, or 1.063 kilograms, of salt to your saltwater tank.

Name:_____ Date:_____

Molarity

Guidelines:

1. You may complete as many of the activities listed as you wish within the time period.
2. You may choose any combination of activities, but **must** complete at least one activity from each topic area.
3. Your goal is 100 points. (This is a grade of 100/100.) You may earn up to _____ points extra credit.
4. You may be as creative as you like within the guidelines listed below.
5. You must show your plan to your teacher by _____ .
6. Activities may be turned in at any time during the working time period. They will be graded and recorded on this sheet as you continue to work, so keep it safe!

Topic	Plan to Do	Activity to Complete	Point Value	Date Completed	Points Earned
Molarity		Write an instruction card that explains how to calculate molarity. Don't forget your units!	10		
		Create a card sort to identify the different parts of a solution.	15		
		Assemble a collage of different solutions; label the solute and solvent of each item you included.	15		
		Perform an original song to help others remember solute, solvent, and their relationship to molarity.	20		
		Invent a class model that shows how molarity represents concentration.	25		
		Develop a social media profile for molarity.	25		
Molarity Calculations		**Problem 1:** A 2.3-liter solution contains 0.32 moles of NaCl. What is its molarity?	5		
		Problem 2: Ocean water has a molarity of about 0.6 M. How many moles of salt would we find in 4 L?	10		
		Problem 3: If the molarity of a 355 mL can of soda is about 0.14 M, how much carbon dioxide is dissolved in the soda?	15		
		Problem 4: A 3 g sugar packet ($C_{12}H_{22}O_{11}$) is emptied into a 400 mL glass of tea. What is the molarity of the solution?	20		
		Problem 5: The molarity of ocean water is about 0.6 M. Your 60-gallon saltwater fish tank is measuring at 0.52 M. How many grams of salt should you add to address this issue?	25		
Any		**Free Choice:** Submit your free choice proposal form for a product of your choice.			
		Total number of points you are planning to earn.		Total points earned:	

I am planning to complete _____ activities that could earn up to a total of _____ points.

Teacher's initials _____ Student's signature _____

Water

20-50-80 Menu

Objectives Covered Through This Menu and These Activities
- Students will be able to describe the unique role of water in solutions in terms of polarity.
- Students will communicate valid conclusions supported by data.
- Students will critique scientific explanations and evaluate the impact of research on scientific thought.

Materials Needed by Students for Completion
- Poster board or large white paper
- Recording software or application (for documentaries)
- Ruler (for comic strips)
- Recycled materials (for models)

Special Notes on the Use of This Menu
- This menu gives students the opportunity to create a documentary. The grading and sharing of these products can often be facilitated by having students prerecord their product using whatever technology is most convenient for the teacher. This allows the teacher to decide when it will be shown as well as keeps the presentation to its intended length. If recording options are limited, this activity can be modified by allowing students to act out the product (like a play) in front of the class.
- This menu asks students to use recycled materials to create their models. This does not mean only plastic and paper; instead, students should focus on using materials in new ways. It works well if a box is started for "recycled" contributions at the beginning of the school year. That way, students always have access to these types of materials.

Time Frame
- 1–2 weeks—Students are given a menu as the unit is started, and the teacher discusses all of the product options on the menu. As the different options are discussed, students will choose the activities they are most interested in completing so that they meet their goal of 100 points. As the lessons progress through the week(s), the teacher and

students refer back to the menu options associated with the content being taught.

- 1–2 days—The teacher chooses an activity or product from the menu to use with the entire class.

Suggested Forms

- All-purpose rubric
- Proposal form for point-based projects

Water

Directions: Choose at least two activities from the menu below. The activities must total 100 points. Place a checkmark next to each box to show which activities you will complete. All activities must be completed by _____ .

---

20 Points

❑ Create an acrostic for the word *water*. Choose phrases for each letter that explain how water's polarity effects its role in solutions.

❑ Draw a comic strip that shows how the polarity of water impacts its ability to create solutions.

---

50 Points

❑ Write a dairy or journal for water's experiences as it encounters both polar and nonpolar substances.

❑ Make and present a model that demonstrates why water is considered the universal solvent.

❑ Propose Three Facts and Fib about water and the unique properties its polarity allows it to demonstrate.

❑ **Free choice on water as a polar substance**—Prepare a proposal form and submit it to your teacher for approval.

---

80 Points

❑ Record a documentary video about the impact the polarity of water has on our world.

❑ Design a social media profile for water. Consider who its friends may be and what types of interactions it could have based on its properties.

Acids and Bases

Three-Topic List Menu

Objectives Covered Through This Menu and These Activities

- Students will be able to define acids and bases.
- Students will be able to distinguish between Arrhenius and Bronsted-Lowry definitions.
- Students will be able to identify strong and weak acids and bases.
- Students will be able to define pH and calculate the pH of a solution using the hydrogen ion concentration.
- Students will be able to define pOH and calculate the pOH of a solution using the hydroxide ion concentration.
- Students will express and manipulate chemical quantities using chemical conventions and mathematical procedures.
- Students will communicate valid conclusions supported by data.
- Students will critique scientific explanations and evaluate the impact of research on scientific thought.

Materials Needed by Students for Completion

- Poster board or large white paper
- Recording software or application (for informational videos)
- Blank index cards (for trading cards and concentration cards)
- Magazines (for collages)
- Large blank lined index cards (for instruction cards)
- Method for recording responses to word problems

Special Notes on the Use of This Menu

- This menu is a product and problem menu; it asks students to not only create products to demonstrate their knowledge but also answer one or more higher level word problems. It is set up in such a way that students will have to complete at least one of the word problems. When introducing this menu, teachers will need to have already determined how they would like these problems completed and recorded for grading. Remember, this is the opportunity to hold high standards when it comes to showing work and defending answers!
- This menu gives students the opportunity to create an informational video. The grading and sharing of these products can often be facil-

itated by having students prerecord their product using whatever technology is most convenient for the teacher. This allows the teacher to decide when it will be shown as well as keeps the presentation to its intended length. If recording options are limited, this activity can be modified by allowing students to act out the product (like a play) in front of the class.

Time Frame

- 1–2 weeks—Students are given the menu as the unit is started, and the guidelines and point expectations are discussed. Students usually will need to earn 100 points for 100%, although there is an opportunity for extra credit if the teacher would like to use another target number. Because this menu covers one topic in depth, the teacher will go over all of the options for the topic being covered and have students place checkmarks in the boxes next to the activities they are most interested in completing. Teachers will need to set aside a few moments to sign the agreement at the bottom of the page with each student. As instruction continues, activities are completed by students and submitted to the teacher for grading.
- 1–2 days—The teacher chooses an activity or product from an objective to use with the entire class during that lesson time.

Suggested Forms

- All-purpose rubric
- Proposal form for point-based products

Answers to Menus Problems

Problem 1: What is the pH of a 2.73×10^{-9} M HCl solution? Is the solution acidic or basic?

$$pH = -\log\left[H^+\right] = -\log\left[2.73 \times 10^{-9}\ M\right]$$
$$pH = 8.56$$

Because the pH is above 7, the solution is basic.

Problem 2: What is the pH of a 3.48×10^{-5} M NaOH solution?

$$pH = -\log\left[OH^-\right] = -\log\left[3.48 \times 10^{-5} \text{ M}\right] \quad pOH = 4.46$$

$$pH + pOH = 14 \quad pH = 14 - pOH$$

$$pH = 14 - 4.46$$

$$pH = 9.54$$

Problem 3: A solution has a pH of 4.87. Find its hydrogen (hydronium) and hydroxide concentrations.

$$[H^+] = 10^{-pH} \quad [OH^-] = 10^{-pOH} \quad pOH = 14 - pH$$

$$[H^+] = 10^{-4.87} \quad [OH^-] = 10^{-9.13}$$

$$\left[H+\right] = 1.35 \times 10^{-5} \text{ M} \quad \left[OH^-\right] = 7.41 \times 10^{-10} \text{ M}$$

Problem 4: Saltwater fish prefer a slightly basic pH between 7.6 and 8.4. When you test your salt water you find the pH to be 6.1. How far off is your hydrogen (hydronium) concentration from the acceptable range?

$$[H^+_{desired}] = 10^{-pH} = 10^{-7.6} = 2.51 \times 10^{-8}$$

$$[H^+_{actual}] = 10^{-pH} = 10^{-6.1} = 7.94 \times 10^{-7}$$

$$[H^+_{actual}] - [H^+_{desired}] = \text{discrepancy in hydrogen concentration}$$

$$7.94 \times 10^{-7} - 2.51 \times 10^{-8} = 7.69 \times 10^{-7} \text{ discrepancy in } \left[H+\right]$$

Name:_____ Date:_____

Acids and Bases

Guidelines:
1. You may complete as many of the activities listed as you wish within the time period.
2. You may choose any combination of activities, but **must** complete at least one activity from each topic area.
3. Your goal is 100 points. (This is a grade of 100/100.) You may earn up to _____ points extra credit.
4. You may be as creative as you like within the guidelines listed below.
5. You must show your plan to your teacher by _____ .
6. Activities may be turned in at any time during the working time period. They will be graded and recorded on this sheet as you continue to work, so keep it safe!

Topic	Plan to Do	Activity to Complete	Point Value	Date Completed	Points Earned
Defining and Identifying Acids and Bases		Assemble a collage of items that are acids and bases. Label each picture as an acid or base.	10		
		There are different definitions for acids and bases, including Arrhenius and Bronsted-Lowry definitions. Draw a three-way Venn diagram to compare these definitions with another common definition.	15		
		Create a set of trading cards for common acids and bases. Be sure to note their status using both Arrhenius and Bronsted-Lowry definitions.	20		
		Consider the different ways that acids and bases are defined, often contradicting each other. Prepare a speech in which you defend which defining system is better.	25		
		Design a social media page for either an Arrhenius or Bronsted-Lowry base.	25		
The pH Scale		Create a set of concentration cards that allow players to match pH values with their concentrations,	10		
		Make a flipbook with 14 flaps. Write the pH scale on the outside and include examples of each pH level on the inside as well as hydrogen (hydronium) and hydroxide concentrations for each.	10		
		Create a folded quiz book that tests your classmates' ability to identify an acid or base and its pH based on information you provide in each question.	15		
		Write Three Facts and a Fib about the pH scale and its relationship to hydrogen (hydronium) concentrations.	15		
		Your friend sent you an e-mail. He just tested the pH of his swimming pool. It is 4.3. Write an e-mail response discussing this pH and, if needed, offer suggestions about swimming in his pool.	20		
		Research different indicators and the chemistry behind how each indicates the pH of a substance. Record an informational video to share your findings.	25		

Name:_____ Date:_____

Acids and Bases, continued

Topic	Plan to Do	Activity to Complete	Point Value	Date Completed	Points Earned
Basic pH Calculations		**Problem 1:** What is the pH of a 2.73×10^{-9} M HCl solution? Is the solution acidic or basic?	20		
		Problem 2: What is the pH of a 3.48×10^{-5} M NaOH solution?	20		
		Problem 3: A solution has a pH of 4.87. Find its hydrogen (hydronium) and hydroxide concentrations.	25		
		Problem 4: Salt water fish prefer a slightly basic pH, between 7.6 and 8.4. When you test your saltwater you find the pH to be 6.1. How far off is your hydrogen (hydronium) concentration from the acceptable range?	30		
Any		**Free Choice:** Submit your free choice proposal form for a product of your choice.			
		Total number of points you are planning to earn.	**Total points earned:**		

I am planning to complete _____ activities that could earn up to a total of _____ points.

Teacher's initials _____ Student's signature _____

CHAPTER 10

Chemical Reactions

 DOI: 10.4324/9781003234357-12

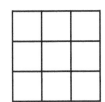

The Mole

Tic-Tac-Toe Menu

Objectives Covered Through This Menu and These Activities
- Students will be able to define and use the concept of a mole.
- Students will be able to calculate the number of atoms or molecules using Avogadro's number.
- Students will express and manipulate chemical quantities using chemical conventions and mathematical procedures.
- Students will communicate valid conclusions supported by data.

Materials Needed by Students for Completion
- Poster board or large white paper
- Materials for board games (folders, colored cards, etc.)
- Microsoft PowerPoint or other slideshow software
- Magazines (for collages)
- Method for recording responses to word problems

Special Notes on the Use of This Menu
- This menu is a product and problem menu; it asks students to not only create products to demonstrate their knowledge but also answer one or more higher level word problems. It is set up in such a way that students will have to complete at least one of the word problems. When introducing this menu, teachers will need to have already determined how they would like these problems completed and recorded for grading. Remember, this is the opportunity to hold high standards when it comes to showing work and defending answers!
- This menu gives students the opportunity to facilitate a class game. The expectation is that all students in the classroom will play an active role in the game. This may mean that the facilitator may need some additional space and time for his or her game. This can take a significant amount of time and organization. It can save time if all of the students who choose to present their game can sign up for a designated day and time that is determined when the menu is distributed.

Time Frame

- 2–3 weeks—Students are given the menu as the unit is started. The teacher will go over all of the options for that content and have students place checkmarks in the boxes that represent the activities they are most interested in completing. As students choose activities, they should complete a column or a row. When students complete this pattern, they have completed one activity from each content area, learning style, or level of Bloom's revised taxonomy, depending on the design of the menu. As the teacher presents lessons throughout the week, he or she should refer back to the menu options associated with that content.
- 1 week—At the start of the unit, the teacher chooses the three activities he or she feels are most valuable for students. Stations can be set up in the classroom. These three activities are available for student choice throughout the week as regular instruction takes place.
- 1–2 days—The teacher chooses an activity from the menu to use with the entire class.

Suggested Forms

- All-purpose rubric
- Student-taught lesson rubric
- Free-choice proposal form

Answers to Menu Problems

Problem 1: Which has a greater mass: 12 mol of salt (NaCl) or 7 mol of silver? Calculate and explain your answer.

$$22.900 \text{ g Na} + 35.453 \text{ g Cl} = 58.4 \text{ g}$$

$$Ag = 107.9 \text{ g}$$

$$12 \text{ mol NaCl} \cdot \frac{58.4 \text{ g NaCl}}{1 \text{ mol NaCl}} = 700.8 \text{ g NaCl or } 701 \text{ g NaCl}$$

$$7 \text{ mol Ag} \cdot \frac{107.9 \text{ g Ag}}{1 \text{ mol Ag}} = 755.3 \text{ g Ag or } 755 \text{ g Ag}$$

Because 7 mol of silver have a mass of 755 g and 12 mol NaCl have a mass of 701 g, 7 mol of silver have a greater mass.

Problem 2: Compare the number of moles in 20 g of hydrogen and 20 L of hydrogen. Which is more? Explain your answer.

$$20 \text{ g H}_2 \cdot \frac{1 \text{ mol H}_2}{2.02 \text{ g H}_2} = 9.9 \text{ mol H}_2$$

$$20 \text{ L H}_2 \cdot \frac{1 \text{ mol H}_2}{22.4 \text{ L}} = 0.893 \text{ mol H}_2$$

Although the values may seem similar at first glance, the answers are quite different. Because one mole of any gas is 22.4 L, it becomes clear that that value will be less than one when compared with the mass of hydrogen.

Problem 3: Which has more molecules: 52.5 L of carbon dioxide (CO_2) or 168. g of chlorine gas (Cl_2)? How many more molecules does the larger substance have?

$$168. \text{ g Cl}_2 \cdot \frac{1 \text{ mol Cl}_2}{70.9 \text{ g Cl}_2} = 2.37 \text{ mol Cl}_2$$

$$52.5 \text{L CO}_2 \cdot \frac{1 \text{ mol CO}_2}{22.4 \text{ LCO}_2} = 2.34 \text{ mol CO}_2$$

$$2.37 \text{ mol Cl}_2 \cdot \frac{6.02 \times 10^{23} \text{ molecules Cl}_2}{1 \text{ mol Cl}_2} = 1.43 \times 10^{24} \text{ molecules Cl}_2$$

$$2.34 \text{ mol CO}_2 \cdot \frac{6.02 \times 10^{23} \text{ molecules CO}_2}{1 \text{ mol CO}_2} = 1.41 \times 10^{24} \text{ molecules CO}_2$$

$$1.43 \times 10^{24} \text{ molecules Cl}_2 - 1.41 \times 10^{24} \text{ molecules CO}_2 = 2 \times 10^{22}$$

$$\text{molecules more of Cl}_2 \text{ than CO}_2$$

The Mole

Directions: Check the boxes you plan to complete. They should form a tic-tac-toe across or down. All products are due by: _____ .

☐ *Defining a Mole* Consider the different values of a mole. Assemble a collage of pictures that represent a mole of different items. Record a measurement on each picture to confirm it is a mole of that substance.	☐ *Problem 1* Which has a greater mass: 12 mol of salt (NaCl) or 7 mol of silver? Calculate and explain your answer.	☐ *Avogadro's Number* Write an original children's book about Avogadro's number in the world around us. Be sure your book could be read and understood by a student in elementary school.
☐ *Avogadro's Number* Create a class game that has your classmates using Avogadro's number to solve chemical word problems.	☐ **Free Choice: Defining a Mole** (Fill out your proposal form before beginning the free choice!)	☐ *Problem 2* Compare the number of moles in 20 g of hydrogen and 20 L of hydrogen. Which is more? Explain your answer.
☐ *Problem 3* Which has more molecules: 52.5 L of carbon dioxide (CO_2) or 168. g of chlorine gas (Cl_2)? How many more molecules does the larger substance have?	☐ *Avogadro's Number* Write and perform an original song about Avogadro's number and its use in chemistry to describe amounts of substances.	☐ *Defining a Mole* A mole is a consistent measurement, yet a mole of one substance may look different that a mole of another substance. Prepare a PowerPoint Presentation to support this statement.

Chemical Reactions

Game Show Menu

Objectives Covered Through This Menu and These Activities

- Students will be able to differentiate among double replacement, synthesis, decomposition, single replacement, and combustion reactions.
- Students will be able to write and balance chemical equations using the law of conservation of mass.
- Students will plan and implement procedures.
- Students will collect data and make measurements with accuracy and precision.
- Students will critique scientific explanations and evaluate the impact of research on scientific thought.

Materials Needed by Students for Completion

- Poster board or large white paper
- Recycled materials (for models)
- Materials for bulletin board display
- Large blank lined index cards (for instruction cards and recipe cards)
- Scrapbooking materials
- Materials for board games (folders, colored cards, etc.)
- Completing Reactions Cube template
- Recording software or application (for videos)
- Blank index cards (for card sorts)
- Microsoft PowerPoint or other slideshow software

Special Notes on the Use of This Menu

- This menu gives students the opportunity to create an experiment. This can take a significant amount of time and organization. It can save time if the experiment is prerecorded (using whatever technology is most convenient) to share at a later time. If the teacher prefers "live" experiments, all of the students who choose to do an experiment can sign up for a designated day and time that is determined when the menu is distributed.
- This menu gives students the opportunity to facilitate a game show. The expectation is that all students in the classroom will have an opportunity to participate in the game show. This may mean that students need some additional time for their product.

- This menu asks students to use recycled materials to create their models. This does not mean only plastic and paper; instead, students should focus on using materials in new ways. It works well if a box is started for "recycled" contributions at the beginning of the school year. That way, students always have access to these types of materials.
- This menu gives students the opportunity to create a video. The grading and sharing of these products can often be facilitated by having students prerecord their product using whatever technology is most convenient for the teacher. This allows the teacher to decide when it will be shown as well as keeps the presentation to its intended length. If recording options are limited, this activity can be modified by allowing students to act out the product (like a play) in front of the class.
- This menu gives students the opportunity to teach a concept. This can take a significant amount of time and organization. It can save time if the students who choose to do a lesson can sign up for a designated day and time that is determined when the menu is distributed.

Time Frame

- 2–3 weeks—Students are given their menu as the unit is started, and the guidelines and point expectations on the back of the menu are discussed. As lessons are taught throughout the unit, students and the teacher can refer back to the options associated with that topic (or column). The teacher will go over all of the options for the topic being covered and have students place checkmarks in the boxes next to the activities they are most interested in completing. As teaching continues over the next 2–3 weeks, activities are discussed, chosen, and submitted for grading.
- 1 week—At the beginning of the unit, the teacher chooses an activity from each area he or she feels would be most valuable for students. Stations can be set up in the classroom, or one of the teacher-selected activities could be provided each day for completion. These activities are available for student choice throughout the week as regular instruction takes place.
- 1–2 days—The teacher chooses an activity from an objective to use with the entire class during that lesson time.

Suggested Forms

- All-purpose rubric
- Student-taught lesson rubric
- Proposal form for point-based products

Guidelines for the Chemical Reactions Game Show Menu

- You must choose at least one activity from each topic area.
- You may not do more than two activities in any one topic area for credit. (You are, of course, welcome to do more than two for your own investigation.)
- Grading will be ongoing, so turn in products as you complete them.
- All free-choice proposals must be turned in and approved *prior* to working on the free choice.
- You must earn **120** points for a 100%. You may earn extra credit up to _____ points.
- You must show your teacher your plan for completion by: _____ .

Chemical Reactions

Types of Reactions	Law of Conservation of Mass	Balancing Reactions	Completing Reactions	Writing Reactions	Points for Each Level
☐ Draw a window pane to show information about each type of reaction we are studying. (10 pts.)	☐ Prepare a recipe card that explains the "ingredients" of this law. (10 pts.)	☐ Build a model that demonstrates why we need to balance chemical reactions. (15 pts.)	☐ Write an instruction card that provides the steps for completing a chemical reaction. Include all types of reactions, including polyatomic ions. (10 pts.)	☐ Develop a reaction scrapbook, in which you write a different type of reaction in words on each page with its reaction and all appropriate chemical symbols including Lewis dot drawings. (15 pts.)	10-15 points
☐ Develop your own way to identify each of the different types of reactions using real-world associations. Record a video in which you share your method. (20 pts.)	☐ Write and perform an original song that explains the importance of the law of conservation of mass. (25 pts.)	☐ Assemble a card sort with examples of balanced and unbalanced reactions. Include all of the different types of reactions. (20 pts.)	☐ Fold two product cubes, one with cations and compounds, the other with anions and compounds, so that when rolled a reaction could be written. Include an answer key for all possible reactions. (25 pts.)	☐ Design a board game in which players must be able to complete reactions, including state symbols, when given the names of the reactants. Include each type of reaction. (25 pts.)	20-25 points
☐ Write and perform a play in which the characters have interactions that represent all of the types of reactions. (30 pts.)	☐ Perform or record an original science experiment that proves the law of conservation of mass. (30 pts.)	☐ Design a PowerPoint game in which players are faced with creative obstacles while practicing balancing equations. (30 pts.)	☐ You have been hired to develop a chemistry-based, entertaining game show based on contestants' skills at completing different chemical reactions. Have fun! (30 pts.)	☐ Prepare a student taught lesson in which you will teacher your classmates all of the aspects of writing and completing reactions. Include all types of reactions, state symbols, and polyatomic ions.	30 points
Free Choice (prior approval) (10–30 pts.)	**Free Choice** (prior approval) (10–30 pts.)	**Free Choice** (prior approval) (10–30 pts.)	**Free Choice** (prior approval) (10–30 pts.)	**Free Choice** (prior approval) (10–30 pts.)	10–30 points
Total:	**Total:**	**Total:**	**Total:**	**Total:**	**Total Grade:**

Reactions Cube

Fold two product cubes, one with cations and compounds, the other with anions and compounds, so that when rolled a reaction could be written. Include an answer key for all possible reactions.

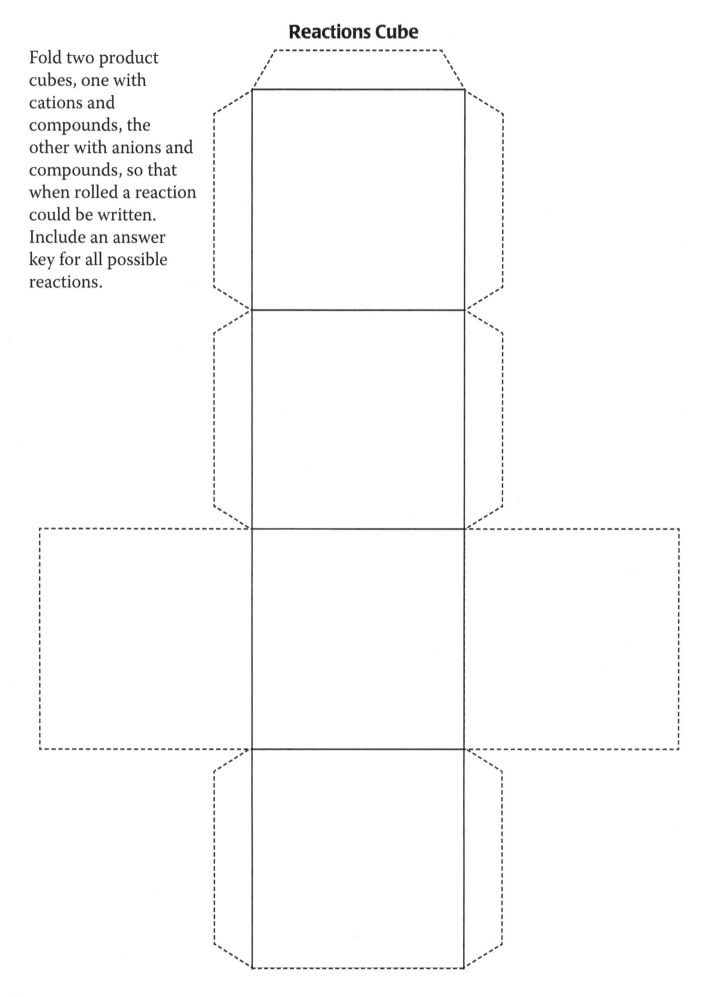

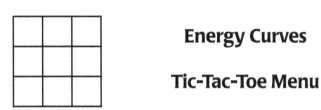

Energy Curves

Tic-Tac-Toe Menu

Objectives Covered Through This Menu and These Activities
- Students will be able to classify reactions as exothermic or endothermic.
- Students will be able to represent energy changes that occur in chemical reactions using thermochemical equations or graphical analysis.

Materials Needed by Students for Completion
- Poster board or large white paper
- Blank index cards (for concentration cards)
- Recording software or application (for videos)
- Scrapbooking materials
- Large blank lined index cards (for instruction cards)

Special Notes on the Use of This Menu
- This menu gives students the opportunity to create videos. The grading and sharing of these products can often be facilitated by having students prerecord their product using whatever technology is most convenient for the teacher. This allows the teacher to decide when it will be shown as well as keeps the presentation to its intended length. If recording options are limited, this activity can be modified by allowing students to act out the product (like a play) in front of the class.
- This menu gives students the opportunity to facilitate a game show. The expectation is that all students in the classroom will have an opportunity to participate in the game show. This may mean that students need some additional time for their product.
- This menu gives students the opportunity to teach a concept. This can take a significant amount of time and organization. It can save time if the students who choose to do a lesson can sign up for a designated day and time that is determined when the menu is distributed.

Time Frame
- 2–3 weeks—Students are given the menu as the unit is started. The teacher will go over all of the options for that content and have students place checkmarks in the boxes that represent the activities they

are most interested in completing. As students choose activities, they should complete a column or a row. When students complete this pattern, they have completed one activity from each content area, learning style, or level of Bloom's revised taxonomy, depending on the design of the menu. As the teacher presents lessons throughout the week, he or she should refer back to the menu options associated with that content.

- 1 week—At the start of the unit, the teacher chooses the three activities he or she feels are most valuable for students. Stations can be set up in the classroom. These three activities are available for student choice throughout the week as regular instruction takes place.
- 1–2 days—The teacher chooses an activity from the menu to use with the entire class.

Suggested Forms

- All-purpose rubric
- Student-taught lesson rubric
- Free-choice proposal form

Name:_____ Date:_____

Energy Curves

Directions: Check the boxes you plan to complete. They should form a tic-tac-toe across or down. All products are due by: _____ .

☐ *Energy Curves*	☐ *Endothermic Reactions*	☐ *Exothermic Reactions*
Prepare a Venn diagram to compare the energy curves of both exothermic and endothermic reactions.	On a poster, draw and label an endothermic energy curve for an endothermic reaction that happens daily.	Record an instructional video to teach your classmates about exothermic energy curves. Use a real-world reaction as an example, and reference catalysts during your explanation.
☐ *Exothermic Reactions*	☐ **Free Choice: Energy Curves** (Fill out your proposal form before beginning the free choice!)	☐ *Endothermic Reactions*
Design a brochure to explain how to create exothermic reaction energy curves given a written reaction and energy change values.		Create a scrapbook of observable endothermic reactions and their energy curves.
☐ *Endothermic Reactions*	☐ *Exothermic Reactions*	☐ *Energy Curves*
You have been given the task of selecting the best online video resource for teaching endothermic reactions. After viewing at least three different resources, record a video reviewing the best source.	Prepare a student-taught lesson in which you teach your classmates how to represent an exothermic equation on a curve. Your explanation should include enthalpy changes.	Create a set of concentration cards in which users match exothermic and endothermic energy curves with their written reactions. Hint: ΔH.

Empirical Formulas, Molecular Formulas, and Percent Composition

Three-Topic List Menu

Objectives Covered Through This Menu and These Activities
- Students will be able to calculate percent composition of compounds.
- Students will be able to differentiate between empirical and molecular formulas.
- Students will express and manipulate chemical quantities using chemical conventions and mathematical procedures.
- Students will communicate valid conclusions supported by data.

Materials Needed by Students for Completion
- Poster board or large white paper
- Microsoft PowerPoint or other slideshow software
- Blank index cards (for card sorts)
- Method for recording responses to word problems

Special Notes on the Use of This Menu
- This menu is a product and problem menu; it asks students to not only create products to demonstrate their knowledge but also answer one or more higher level word problems. It is set up in such a way that students will have to complete at least one of the word problems. When introducing this menu, teachers will need to have already determined how they would like these problems completed and recorded for grading. Remember, this is the opportunity to hold high standards when it comes to showing work and defending answers!

Time Frame
- 1–2 weeks—Students are given the menu as the unit is started, and the guidelines and point expectations are discussed. Students usually will need to earn 100 points for 100%, although there is an opportunity for extra credit if the teacher would like to use another target number. Because this menu covers one topic in depth, the teacher will go over all of the options for the topic being covered and have students place checkmarks in the boxes next to the activities they are most interested in completing. Teachers will need to set aside a few

moments to sign the agreement at the bottom of the page with each student. As instruction continues, activities are completed by students and submitted to the teacher for grading.

- 1–2 days—The teacher chooses an activity or product from an objective to use with the entire class during that lesson time.

Suggested Forms

- All-purpose rubric
- Proposal form for point-based products

Answers to Menu Problems

Problem 1: Calculate the percent of hydrogen and oxygen in water.

$$\text{Percent composition} = \frac{\text{mass of element}}{\text{mass of compound}} \times 100$$

$$\text{Hydrogen}: \frac{2.016 \text{ g H}_2}{18.01 \text{ g H}_2\text{O}} \times 100 = 11.2\%$$

$$\text{Oxygen}: \frac{15.99 \text{ g O}}{18.01 \text{ g H}_2\text{O}} \times 100 = 88.8\%$$

Problem 2: If a 14-karat gold ring is 58.3% gold, how many grams of gold would there be in a ring with a mass of 5.21 g?

$$5.21 \text{ g ring} \cdot \frac{58.3}{100} = 3.04 \text{ g of gold}$$

Problem 3: Which element represents most of baking soda (sodium hydrogen carbonate)?

Baking soda is $NaHCO_3$.

$$\text{Sodium}: \frac{22.99 \text{ g}}{84.10 \text{ g}} \times 100 = 27.34\%$$

$$\text{Hydrogen:}\ \frac{1.008\ g}{84.10\ g}\times100=1.200\%$$

$$\text{Carbon:}\ \frac{12.01\ g}{84.10\ g}\times100=14.28\%$$

$$\text{Oxygen:}\ \frac{48\ g}{84.10\ g}\times100=57.19\%$$

Oxygen represents most of baking soda.

Problem 4: How many grams of oxygen are in 20 g of sugar $(C_{12}H_{22}O_{11})$?

$$\text{Oxygen:}\ \frac{176\ g\ O}{342\ g\ C_{12}H_{22}O_{11}}\times100=51.42\%$$

If sugar is 51.42% oxygen and we have 20 g of sugar, then we can calculate the grams of oxygen in 20 g of sugar.

$$\frac{51.42}{100}\times20\ g=10.28\ g\ \text{of carbon in 20 g of sugar}$$

Problem 5: The empirical formula of a compound is CH_2O. If its molar mass is 180 grams, what is its molecular formula?

Empirical Formula Mass = 1 Carbon + 2 Hydrogens + 1 Oxygen

$$=12\ g+2.02\ g+16\ g$$

$$=30.02\ g$$

$$\frac{180\ g\ \left(\text{molar mass}\right)}{30.02\ g\ \left(\text{empirical mass}\right)}=6$$

The molecular formula is $C_6H_{12}O_6$.

Problem 6: What is the empirical formula if a compound consists of 21.2% nitrogen, 6.10% hydrogen, 24.2% sulfur, and 48.5% oxygen?

$$\text{Nitrogen}: 21.2 \text{ g N} \cdot \frac{1 \text{ mol N}}{14.01 \text{ g N}} = \frac{1.5}{0.75} = 2$$

$$\text{Hydrogen}: 6.10 \text{ g H} \cdot \frac{1 \text{ mol H}}{1.01 \text{ g H}} = \frac{6.03}{0.75} = 8$$

$$\text{Sulfur}: 24.2 \text{ g S} \cdot \frac{1 \text{ mol S}}{32.1 \text{ g S}} = \frac{0.75}{0.75} = 1$$

$$\text{Oxygen}: 48.5 \text{ g O} \cdot \frac{1 \text{ mol O}}{16 \text{ g O}} = \frac{3.03}{0.75} = 4$$

The empirical formula is $N_2H_8SO_4$.

Problem 7: A compound with a mass of 510 g contains 89.52 g of sodium, 202.47 g of chromium, and 218.01 g of oxygen. What is its empirical formula?

$$\text{Sodium}: \frac{89.52 \text{ g}}{510 \text{ g}} \cdot 100 = 17.55 \cdot \frac{1 \text{ mol Na}}{22.99 \text{ g Na}} = \frac{0.76 \text{ mol Na}}{0.76 \text{ mol}} = 1$$

$$\text{Chromium}: \frac{202.47 \text{ g}}{510 \text{ g}} \cdot 100 = 39.7 \cdot \frac{1 \text{ mol Cr}}{52 \text{ g Cr}} = \frac{0.76 \text{ mol Cr}}{0.76 \text{ mol}} = 1$$

$$\text{Oxygen}: \frac{218.01 \text{ g}}{510 \text{ g}} \cdot 100 = 42.7 \cdot \frac{1 \text{ mol O}}{16 \text{ g O}} = \frac{2.7 \text{ mol O}}{0.76 \text{ mol}} = 3.5$$

Because we cannot have 3.5 as a subscript, we must multiply by 2. The empirical formula is $Na_2Cr_2O_7$.

Problem 8: A scientist collects 10.76 g of an unknown substance. It contains 4.164 g of carbon, 1.035 g of hydrogen, and 5.550 g of oxygen. Its molar mass is 186 g. What are its empirical and molecular formulas?

Calculate the empirical formula:

$$\text{Carbon:} \quad \frac{4.164 \text{ g C}}{10.76 \text{ g}} \cdot 100 = 38.7\% \cdot \frac{1 \text{ mol C}}{12.05 \text{ g C}} = 3.22 = 1$$

$$\text{Hydrogen:} \quad \frac{1.035 \text{ g H}}{10.76 \text{ g}} \cdot 100 = 9.62\% \cdot \frac{1 \text{ mol H}}{1.01 \text{ g H}} = \frac{9.52}{3.22} = 3$$

$$\text{Oxygen:} \quad \frac{5.550 \text{ g O}}{10.76 \text{ g}} \cdot 100 = 51.6\% \cdot \frac{1 \text{ mol}}{16 \text{ g}} = \frac{3.22}{3.22} = 1$$

The empirical formula is CH_3O, which is 31.03 g.

Calculate the molecular formula:

$$\frac{186 \text{ g}}{31.03 \text{ g}} = 6$$

The molecular formula is $C_6H_{18}O_6$.

Name:_____ Date:_____

Empirical Formulas, Molecular Formulas, and Percent Composition

Guidelines:

1. You may complete as many of the activities listed as you wish within the time period.
2. You may choose any combination of activities, but **must** complete at least one activity from each topic area.
3. Your goal is 100 points. (This is a grade of 100/100.) You may earn up to _____ points extra credit.
4. You may be as creative as you like within the guidelines listed below.
5. You must show your plan to your teacher by _____ .
6. Activities may be turned in at any time during the working time period. They will be graded and recorded on this sheet as you continue to work, so keep it safe!

Topic	Plan to Do	Activity to Complete	Point Value	Date Completed	Points Earned
Empirical and Molecular Formulas		Make a card sort to separate real-world examples of molecular and empirical formulas.	15		
		Complete a Venn diagram to compare empirical and molecular formulas.	20		
		Can an empirical and molecular formula be the same? Prepare a PowerPoint presentation to answer this question.	25		
Percent Composition		**Problem 1:** Calculate the percent of hydrogen and oxygen in water.	10		
		Problem 2: If a 14-karat gold ring is 58.3% gold, how many grams of gold would there be in a ring with a mass of 5.21 g?	15		
		Problem 3: Which element represents most of baking soda (sodium hydrogen carbonate)?	20		
		Problem 4: How many grams of oxygen are in 20 g of sugar ($C_{12}H_{22}O_{11}$)?	20		
Calculating Empirical and Molecular Formulas		**Problem 5:** The empirical formula of a compound is CH_2O. If its molar mass is 180 g, what is its molecular formula?	10		
		Problem 6: What is the empirical formula if a compound consists of 21.2% nitrogen, 6.10% hydrogen, 24.2% sulfur, and 48.5% oxygen?	15		
		Problem 7: A compound with a mass of 510 g contains 89.52 g of sodium, 202.47 g of chromium, and 218.01 g of oxygen. What is its empirical formula?	20		
		Problem 8: A scientist collects 10.76 g of an unknown substance. It contains 4.164 g of carbon, 1.035 g of hydrogen, and 5.550 g of oxygen. Its molar mass is 186 g. What are its empirical and molecular formulas?	25		
Any		**Free Choice:** Submit your free choice proposal form for a product of your choice.			
		Total number of points you are planning to earn.		**Total points earned:**	

I am planning to complete _____ activities that could earn up to a total of _____ points.

Teacher's initials _____ Student's signature _____

Nuclear Chemistry

Three-Topic List Menu

Objectives Covered Through This Menu and These Activities

- Students will compare fission and fusion reactions.
- Students will be able to describe the characteristics of alpha, beta, and gamma radioactive decay processes in terms of balanced nuclear equations.
- Students will express and manipulate chemical quantities using chemical conventions and mathematical procedures.
- Students will communicate valid conclusions supported by data.

Materials Needed by Students for Completion

- Poster board or large white paper
- Materials for three-dimensional timelines
- Microsoft PowerPoint or other slideshow software
- Coat hangers (for mobiles)
- String (for mobiles)
- Blank index cards (for mobiles)
- Materials for board games (folders, colored cards, etc.)
- Recording software or application (for news reports)

Special Notes on the Use of This Menu

- This menu is a product and problem menu; it asks students to not only create products to demonstrate their knowledge but also answer one or more higher level word problems. It is set up in such a way that students will have to complete at least one of the word problems. When introducing this menu, teachers will need to have already determined how they would like these problems completed and recorded for grading. Remember, this is the opportunity to hold high standards when it comes to showing work and defending answers!
- This menu gives students the opportunity to create a news report. The grading and sharing of these products can often be facilitated by having students prerecord their product using whatever technology is most convenient for the teacher. This allows the teacher to decide when it will be shown as well as keeps the presentation to its intended length. If recording options are limited, this activity can be modified

by allowing students to act out the product (like a play) in front of the class.

Time Frame

- 1–2 weeks—Students are given the menu as the unit is started, and the guidelines and point expectations are discussed. Students usually will need to earn 100 points for 100%, although there is an opportunity for extra credit if the teacher would like to use another target number. Because this menu covers one topic in depth, the teacher will go over all of the options for the topic being covered and have students place checkmarks in the boxes next to the activities they are most interested in completing. Teachers will need to set aside a few moments to sign the agreement at the bottom of the page with each student. As instruction continues, activities are completed by students and submitted to the teacher for grading.
- 1–2 days—The teacher chooses an activity or product from an objective to use with the entire class during that lesson time.

Suggested Forms

- All-purpose rubric
- Proposal form for point-based products

Answers to Menu Problems

Problem 1: Write a balanced nuclear equation that shows how proactinium-229 goes through two alpha decays and francium-221 is formed.

$$^{229}_{91}\text{Pa} \rightarrow \, ^{225}_{89}\text{Ac} + \, ^{4}_{2}\text{He} \rightarrow \, ^{221}_{87}\text{Fr} + \, ^{4}_{2}\text{He}$$

Problem 2: Thorium-231 is produced from an alpha and then a beta decay. What was its parent substance?

$$^{231}_{90}\text{Th} + \, ^{0}_{-1}\text{e} \leftarrow \, ^{231}_{89}\text{Ac} + \, ^{4}_{2}\text{He} \leftarrow \, ^{235}_{91}\text{Pa}$$

The parent substance was proactinium-235.

Problem 3: Radon-222 goes through eight steps to become stable. Write a balanced nuclear equation representing the following decays: two alphas, three betas, one alpha, one beta, one alpha.

$$^{222}_{86}Rn \rightarrow {}^{4}_{2}He + {}^{218}_{84}Po \rightarrow {}^{4}_{2}He + {}^{214}_{82}Pb \rightarrow {}^{0}_{-1}e + {}^{214}_{83}Bi \rightarrow {}^{0}_{-1}e + {}^{214}_{84}Po \rightarrow$$

$$^{0}_{-1}e + {}^{214}_{85}At \rightarrow {}^{4}_{2}He + {}^{210}_{83}Bi \rightarrow {}^{0}_{-1}e + {}^{210}_{84}Po \rightarrow {}^{4}_{2}He + {}^{206}_{82}Pb$$

Problem 4: Uranium-238 goes through 14 decays before becoming stable. Write a balanced nuclear equation that shows Uranium-238 going through these decays in order: one alpha, two betas, five alphas, two betas, one alpha, two betas, and a final alpha decay. What is your final product?

$$^{238}_{92}U \rightarrow {}^{4}_{2}He + {}^{234}_{90}Th \rightarrow {}^{0}_{-1}e + {}^{234}_{91}Pa \rightarrow {}^{0}_{-1}e + {}^{234}_{92}U \rightarrow {}^{4}_{2}He + {}^{230}_{90}Th \rightarrow {}^{4}_{2}He + {}^{226}_{88}Ra \rightarrow$$

$$^{4}_{2}He + {}^{222}_{86}Rn \rightarrow {}^{4}_{2}He + {}^{218}_{84}Po \rightarrow {}^{4}_{2}He + {}^{214}_{82}Pb \rightarrow {}^{0}_{-1}e + {}^{214}_{83}Bi \rightarrow {}^{0}_{-1}e + {}^{214}_{84}Po \rightarrow {}^{4}_{2}He +$$

$$^{210}_{82}Pb \rightarrow {}^{0}_{-1}e + {}^{210}_{83}Bi \rightarrow {}^{0}_{-1}e + {}^{210}_{84}Po \rightarrow {}^{4}_{2}He + {}^{206}_{82}Pb$$

The final product is lead-206.

Name:_____ Date:_____

Nuclear Chemistry

Guidelines:

1. You may complete as many of the activities listed as you wish within the time period.
2. You may choose any combination of activities, but **must** complete at least one activity from each topic area.
3. Your goal is 100 points. (This is a grade of 100/100.) You may earn up to _____ points extra credit.
4. You may be as creative as you like within the guidelines listed below.
5. You must show your plan to your teacher by _____ .
6. Activities may be turned in at any time during the working time period. They will be graded and recorded on this sheet as you continue to work, so keep it safe!

Topic	Plan to Do	Activity to Complete	Point Value	Date Completed	Points Earned
Fission and Fusion		Complete a thematic Venn diagram to compare the processes of fission and fusion.	15		
		A new book has been written on the chemistry of nuclear fission. Design a book cover for this new book.	20		
		Build a three-dimensional timeline for research in the areas of fission and fusion.	20		
		Interview a researcher in the field of nuclear fission or fusion. Prepare a poster or PowerPoint to share your findings.	25		
Decays		Assemble a mobile with information about each of the different radioactive decay processes.	10		
		Draw a mind map with *radioactive decay* in the middle. Be sure to include all pertinent information.	15		
		Invent a board game in which players get to experience the impact of different radioactive decay processes.	20		
		Someone has reported a large release of alpha particles. Record a news report addressing the incident and offering safety tips.	25		
Nuclear reactions		**Problem 1:** Write a balanced nuclear equation that shows how pro-actinium-229 goes through two alpha decays and francium 221 is formed.	10		
		Problem 2: Thorium-231 is produced from an alpha and then a beta decay. What was its parent substance?	15		
		Problem 3: Radon-222 goes through eight steps to become stable. Write a balanced nuclear equation representing the following decays: two alphas, three betas, one alpha, one beta, one alpha.	25		
		Problem 4: Uranium-238 goes through 14 decays before becoming stable. Write a balanced nuclear equation that shows Uranium-238 going through these decays in order: one alpha, two betas, five alphas, two betas, one alpha, two betas, and a final alpha decay. What is your final product? How is it different from Uranium-238?	30		
Any		**Free Choice:** Submit your free choice proposal form for a product of your choice.			
		Total number of points you are planning to earn.	**Total points earned:**		

I am planning to complete _____ activities that could earn up to a total of _____ points.

Teacher's initials _____ Student's signature _____

References

Anderson, L., & Krathwohl, D. R. (Eds.). (2001). *A taxonomy for learning, teaching, and assessing: A revision of Bloom's taxonomy of educational objectives* (Complete ed.). New York, NY: Longman.

Deci, E. L., Vallerand, R. J., Pelletier, L. G., & Ryan, R. M. (1991). Motivation and education: The self-determination perspective. *Educational Psychologist, 26,* 325–346.

Dunn, R., & Honigsfeld, A. (2013). Learning styles: what we know and what we need. *The Educational Forum, 77,* 225–232. doi:10.1080/00 131725.2013.765328

Flowerday, T., & Schraw, G. (2003). Effect of choice on cognitive and affective engagement. *The Journal of Educational Research, 96,* 207–215. doi:10.1080/00220670309598810

Keen, D. (2001). *Talent in the new millennium: Report on year one of the programme.* Paper presented at the meeting of the Australian Association for Research in Education, Perth.

Komarraju, M., Karau, S. J., Schmeck, R. R., & Avdic, A. (2011). The Big Five personality traits, learning styles, and academic achievement. *Personality and Individual Differences, 51,* 472–477. http://dx.doi.org/10.1016/j.paid.2011.04.019

Litman, J. (2005). Epistemic curiosity, feeling-of-knowing, and exploratory behaviour. *Cognition & Emotion, 19,* 559–582.

Magner, L. (2000). Reaching all children through differentiated assessment: The 2-5-8 plan. *Gifted Child Today, 23*(3), 48–50.

Patall, E. A. (2013). Constructing motivation through choice, interest, and interestingness. *Journal of Educational Psychology, 105,* 522–534. doi:10.1037/a0030307

Ricca, J. (1984). Learning styles and preferred instructional strategies of gifted students. *Gifted Child Quarterly, 28,* 121–126.

Robinson, J., Patall, E. A., & Cooper, H. (2008). The effects of choice on intrinsic motivation and related outcomes: a meta-analysis of research findings. *Psychological Bulletin, 134,* 270–300.

Sagan, L. (2010). Students' choice: Recommendations for environmental and instructional changes in school. *The Clearing House: A Journal of Educational Strategies, Issues and Ideas, 83,* 217–222. doi:10.1080/00098650903505407

Snyder, R. (1999). The relationship between learning styles/multiple intelligences and academic achievement of high school students. *The High School Journal, 83*(2), 11–20.

About the Author

After teaching science for more than 15 years, both overseas and in the U.S., **Laurie E. Westphal, Ed.D.,** now works as an independent gifted education and science consultant nationwide. She enjoys developing and presenting staff development on low-stress differentiation strategies and using menus for various districts and conferences, working with teachers to assist them in planning and developing lessons to meet the needs of their advanced students. Laurie currently resides in Houston, TX, and has made it her goal to convert as many teachers as she can to the differentiated lifestyle in the classroom and to share her vision for real-world, product-based lessons that help all students become critical thinkers and effective problem solvers. She is the author of the Differentiating Instruction With Menus series as well as *Hands-On Physical Science* and *Science Dictionary for Kids*.

Common Core Standards and Next Generation Science Standards

This b ook a ligns with an e xtensive n umber of t he C ommon C ore State Standards and Next Generation Science Standards. Please visit https://www.routledge.com/ccss.aspx to download a complete packet of the standards that align with each individual menu in this book.